What's Your Soul Goal... silly?

DR. JOSHUA HEINES

1 MESSAGE
m e d i a
.com

ISBN: 0-692-84644-1
ISBN-13: 978-0-692-84644-5
1. Christian living. I. Title.

To order copies of this book in bulk quantities,
please contact us by email at team@1messagemedia.com
or
by visiting www.SoulGoalBook.com

DEDICATION

This book is dedicated to all those who have yet to hear the Good News message of Jesus Christ. May this book in some way be a catalyst to someone bringing that message to you.

CONTENTS

ACKNOWLEDGMENTS

Thank you to my amazing wife, Diane. Although this book was written by me, it is an extension of the commitment my wife and I have made to the mission of reaching others together.

To my daughter, Faith. Through it all God has given us a representation of his Love, which is you. You are a shining light and true inspiration in my life. May this book one day be a representation of the rich heritage God has given you.

INTRODUCTION

Have you ever had one of those thoughts that seemingly came from nowhere that you just can't get rid of? It's not necessarily a bad thought, just a random and annoying one. No matter what you do, the thought plagues your mind over the course of a day, a week, or even worse…several weeks or more. It's the kind of thought that randomly and annoyingly keeps coming back even though you want nothing to do with it. Just when you think it's gone, surprise, here it comes again. Eventually, after ignoring the thought long enough, it is gone. You can't really remember when it left; it just did. In fact, you may even be able to relate to what I am describing because it has happened to you in the past, but the thought you had that kept returning is so long gone, that right now you can't even remember what it was. You just know you've experienced that before.

I have had these kinds of thoughts come to me from time to time in my life, but never like one did recently. When these kinds of lingering thoughts have come to my mind in the past, one of two things would eventually happen. I would either ignore the thought until it went away (which I openly admit is what would happen most of the time), or I would pray about it and see if God was trying to show me something (I should have done this more often).

Recently, one phrase started coming to my mind over and over. It would not go away, and at first, I definitely wanted it too. Why? Because I had a pretty good idea of what it meant, but I certainly didn't want to spend much time thinking about it, even though as a Christian I knew I probably should.

Simply put, if it did mean what I had a feeling it meant, I didn't want to deal with it because doing so would require me to reflect upon everything my life stood for. It would cause me to dig deep into scripture for truth that I knew would challenge my inner being and earthly existence to the very core. I didn't want to be challenged like that. I had too much going on… too many goals to reach. I was working hard trying to accomplish personal and business goals, all while trying to live my life the best I could as a Christian living in the world, but not of the world. Sound familiar???

So, when this thought came and kept coming back, at first I did what I most commonly did when this happened to me in the past, I tried to ignore it. I hoped that if I ignored it long enough, it would eventually just go away like so many lingering thoughts had done before. After over a month of ignoring, the phrase persisted in my mind. Now this had never happened to me before. Not only was it still there, it was now coming back more frequently and even louder than when it started out. You know… the thought that is so loud in your mind that you can't even think about anything else. The thought that crowds every other thought out and makes them as a distant muffle in the background of your mind. This was that kind of thought, and even though I wanted it too, it wasn't going away any time soon.

Finally, enough was enough. I realized I could no longer ignore this one. Ignoring it was not going to make it go away, it was only going to make it worse. I knew I was out of options. There was only one thing left to do… and I must say, I was not that thrilled about doing it. I had to face the phrase and everything that came with it head-on. No more thought evasion.

I approached cautiously and with great hesitation. As I alluded to before, I had a slight suspicion that if I really prayed to God and sought out his guidance, understanding, and truth in regards to this phrase, it would most likely rock my world to the inner core. It would cause me to never be the same. It would cause me to change the way I lived my life and I wasn't quite sure if I wanted to do that. Nevertheless, the phrase remained inside of me, growing louder and louder, stronger and stronger, more frequent and more intense day by day. It was time to face the phrase…What's Your Soul Goal?

CHAPTER ONE

Drawing a Blank

It was coming up on the end of December. As many business managers and owners do around this time of year, I was looking at my business goals I had set for myself to reach that year. I was reflecting upon things I did well, things I didn't do so well, goals I had reached, and goals I failed to reach. It was a process I had grown quite accustomed too as a business owner. I had learned over the past several years that this process was vital to my success in evaluating my actions, identifying strengths and weaknesses, and keeping me on the path to improvement and success.

After spending some time reflecting back over the year that was coming to an end, the next step in this process would be to start setting goals for the next year. Identifying what had worked really well for the business was crucial, but I also made changes to other things that didn't work so well. With this formula, I would then look to the future, towards the upcoming year and set some specific goals that we would work towards.

However, this particular December was different. As I began to spend time in prayer thinking about and asking God what goals I should set for the upcoming year, I got nothing. Total blank. At first I wasn't too concerned, as from past experiences for me, this process could take anywhere from several days to over a week. But when

New Year's Eve was suddenly upon me and I was still drawing a total blank, I knew something was up.

Getting concerned, I called a Christian friend of mine who was my mentor in business and explained the situation to him. I asked him what I should do. He told me that it was quite unusual, but not to worry about it and just keep doing what I was doing. So, I did.

Even though it was extremely uncomfortable (and I thought foolish to do), I started off the first of January that year with not one single goal for my business. Weeks went by and I continued to pray and seek the Lord for goals and direction for my business as a Christian business owner, but the response... nothing, a total blank.

Becoming increasingly frustrated with every day that went by, I couldn't understand why. Why wasn't God answering me? Why wasn't God helping me? Why, when I even thought about setting goals, my mind completely drew a blank as if I couldn't think at all?

Then, it suddenly dawned on me. In my state of increasing frustration, with a lack of goals and direction... BAM, the phrase that had persisted and wouldn't leave my mind hit me...

CHAPTER TWO

The Phrase

What's your Soul Goal????

What is that?!?! That was my exact initial reaction to this phrase. I was in shock. After all, up until this time, I do not think I had ever even heard this phrase before in my life. It seemingly came out of nowhere and made its home in my mind. It demanded an answer and wasn't going away until it got one.

When the phrase kept coming back to my mind, time and time again, over the first few days, I vividly remember responding back with the answer of: "what do you mean, what is my Soul Goal? What is that? Soul Goal. What in the world is a Soul Goal?" It felt as if I was having a conversation with God himself, and even though I was responding this way, as a Christian I already had a pretty good idea of what the phrase meant. However, since I had never heard this phrase and no one had ever asked me this question before, I believe I was still initially in a state of shock at the magnitude of the question.

Here I was trying to come up with all these other goals in my life and getting nowhere; when now I was confronted with a question in regards to a goal that: 1. I had never thought about setting before and 2. I knew perhaps was more important than any other goal I could possibly have in my life.

Now you can maybe understand why I just wanted the phrase to go away. I knew that going any further into prayer, discovery, revelation, and understanding about "what's your Soul Goal?" would most likely challenge me to my very core and cause me to make some huge changes in the way I lived my life. And That Is Exactly What It Did. I must caution you that reading any further may do the same for you too! Nevertheless, I challenge you to keep reading…

Goals. Goals. Goals.

From being an accomplished pilot, to training for and running two full marathons (each 26.2 miles), to earning a doctorate degree, I knew what it meant to set goals and work towards accomplishing them. I had set a lot of goals in my lifetime, taken a lot of actions towards achieving them, and ultimately accomplished many of them. However, I had never even thought about having a Soul Goal.

At the time this phrase came to me, I had just spent the last three years of my life planning for, starting, and running my own business. If you have ever started and ran your own business before, you know that setting goals and working towards them daily, is vital to the success of starting and running a business. For those of you who have never started and ran your own business before, let me just say, the word goal becomes so much a part of your life, that you literally feel like you eat, drink, sleep, weep, run, walk… and constantly think about GOALS. Daily, weekly, monthly, yearly. Goals. Goals. Goals. At least that's what I did.

Mastering the simple process of goal-setting is what can literally determine the level of success you have in accomplishing your desires in life. Many of the people we look up to around the world (that are considered highly successful people) have mastered the process of goal-setting and taking action steps toward achieving those goals. I have learned that setting goals in my life is extremely important. However, I did not have a Soul Goal.

I was constantly setting goals, accomplishing them, and then setting even bigger ones… and accomplishing them. It was a constant, on-going cycle. If I was having a difficult time accomplishing a goal, I would evaluate all my activities that I was doing to reach the goal. Were any of my actions actually keeping me from reaching the goal? I would go into a mode of evaluation and refining my actions to enable me to reach my goal. After all, if I wasn't reaching my goals doing what I was doing, I definitely did not want to keep doing the same actions. **Same actions equals same results, and if the results are less than reaching my goal, my actions needed to change.**

This was my life. Goals. Goals. Goals.

Don't Ask Me That Question

So I approached this phrase slowly, with tremendous apprehension as I had a sense of what this phrase was requiring me to answer. I had never answered this question before. I had never even put much thought to it. I knew I did not have this goal set in my life and now I had a strong suspicion that I should.

I spent time seeking the Lord for answers and revelation as to what exactly he meant by this phrase, "What's Your Soul Goal?" but to be quite honest, I already knew the answer. It was as if I didn't want THE meaning of this phrase to be the real meaning, so I kept stalling and pressing God for more, in hopes that what I already knew was being asked of me would somehow magically turn into a different question. I was in denial and I thought, "God, don't ask me that question."

Have you ever done that with God? Have you ever delayed in answering God when he asks you a question or tells you to do something in hopes that it will somehow go away or turn into something that's more comfortable for you? Well, that's what I was doing and after some time of stalling and delaying, what I knew was being asked of me was not changing. God's challenge to me was serious and he wasn't going to let me off-the-hook on this one. He required an answer and whether I gave it to him now or later, I was still responsible for the answer.

The initial meaning of the phrase "What's Your Soul Goal?" that I had spent so much time and effort trying to avoid, I knew was in reference to the number of souls that I wanted to win in my lifetime. Simply put, this phrase was in reference to my personal goal for reaching and winning souls with the message of the Gospel. What was my Soul Goal? More specifically, what was the number of souls that I am working towards reaching and winning in my lifetime? When I get to the end of my life and look back, how many souls saved through my life lived would be a fulfilling number to me? How many souls did I feel responsible for winning? How many souls did I think I could win in my lifetime with God's help? It was as if God was asking me: "How many souls can you believe me for in your lifetime?"

As a Christian, and knowing how important my relationship with God is to me, I naturally wanted others to live in daily relationship with God too. It hurt me to see people trying to go through life on their own while rejecting God. It hurt me to see people on the wrong road towards eternity. I had a desire to see others receive salvation. I had a desire to see souls won for the Kingdom of God and to see people receive forgiveness of their sins and the promise of eternal life. Furthermore, I knew as a Christian, God had given me the mission and responsibility to tell others about the message of salvation, just like he has given to every Christian. However, I did not have a specific goal for the number of souls, the number of people that I was intentionally and actively working towards reaching. And seemingly, that is exactly what this phrase, this question, was asking me to have.

Now you can see why I approached this phrase slowly with great apprehension. Internally, I knew answering the question with sincerity may cause me to have a greater sense of personal responsibility to the mission that God had already given me as a Christian in a way that setting specific goals tends to have. Even though I knew God has called every Christian to "go and make disciples," setting a specific number goal to that mission brings such a greater sense of responsibility and accountability to, if nobody else, myself. A responsibility and accountability that I must admit I wasn't sure if I wanted to willingly embrace.

However, after stalling, delaying and questioning God, I had gotten to a point where I was willing to answer the question I most certainly knew was being asked of me. What's Your Soul Goal?

Like so many people would respond, I initially responded like this: "God, I can believe you for a lot of souls. You are such a big God and therefore, I know you can use me to win so many souls for you. I am ready. I want to win a lot of souls for you. Use me in a big way to reach as many souls for you as you want."

Have you ever done that? In an attempt to appease God, have you ever answered God so foolishly, that when you look back at the situation you become so embarrassed at yourself?

Well, as foolish as it was, that was my response. That vague, lousy, non-specific response was almost automatic once I decided to answer the question of "What is my Soul Goal?" and that's embarrassing. After all, like so many other people I know, I could come up with very specific goals for everything else in my life. I had goals for my family life, running marathons, which countries I wanted to visit in my lifetime, graduating college, income, career, my business goals, etc. However, when it came to setting a goal for souls, I responded with such a vague answer, it was a joke to even consider it a goal. How foolish of me to think that such a vague answer, to such an important question, would even remotely be acceptable to God. And of course, it wasn't.

It was as if God didn't even hear that answer. What do I mean? Well, the phrase "What's Your Soul Goal?" still kept repeating over and over in my mind. So, I responded the same way again. Not wanting to *really* set a specific goal (even though my answer was total foolishness compared to any specific goal I would set for my business), I was hoping that in some way, my answer would be acceptable. I secretly hoped that the phrase would just go away so I could get on with running my business and living my life.

Nevertheless, the phrase persisted. And it became quite clear one day just how wrong I was with my vague answer, when I felt as if the Lord himself asked me: "you would never set that kind of non-specific goal for your business, why would you do it for souls?"

In an instant, I was crushed. Talk about perspective. I had just gotten one. I had now come face-to-face with the reality of my life as a Christian that I was hoping to avoid. As a Christian I have a mission. And the question requires a specific answer.

I eventually did give a specific answer. And when I did, the phrase immediately went away. God even confirmed the answer I gave was correct through a series of most unusual events. More on that later.

The following is what I have come to know about what it means to have a Soul Goal, how it pertains to scripture, why you would want one, and how you can implement one into your life as a Christian as well...

CHAPTER THREE

What it Means to Have a Soul Goal
Part 1

And the LORD God formed man of the dust of the ground, and breathed into his nostrils the breath of life; and man became a living soul.

(Genesis 2:7 KJV)

Understand, you could spend countless hours, even years, studying about and trying to comprehend the complexity of God's human creations: the man and woman. In doing so, you will most inevitably come to the conclusion that no matter how long you study or how hard you try, the more you know, the more you know there is to know. Simply put, in this life you will never know all there is to know about humankind.

With that said, understand that from a simplistic point of view, God created you and I with a soul, spirit and physical body. Moreover, it could be said that a soul is the mind, will, and emotions of a person. With this basic understanding, you could think in terms of a Soul Goal as having a goal to reach or win the mind, will, and emotions of a certain number of people on earth throughout your lifetime. Furthermore, as a Christian, you could also say a Soul Goal is a goal to reach a certain number of peoples' *mind* with the message of the Gospel, bringing them to a crossroad where they must choose with their own free *will* whether or not they will accept salvation through Jesus Christ, and therefore whether or not they will have *emotions* that reflect their acceptance and love for the Lord.

Soul Goal Clarification

Just to be absolutely clear…for the sake of simplicity and the purposes of this book, think in terms of a Soul Goal as your goal for the number of people you want to reach or win as a Christian with the message of salvation and reconciliation unto God through Jesus Christ for the Kingdom of God throughout your entire lifetime. In other words, you should think of it as a long-term, life-long goal with a specific number.

End of Life Looking Back

Sometimes imagining yourself in the future looking back upon your life helps you to gain clarity on what really matters to you, or at least should. Many times, we imagine what we want our lives to be like 10, 15, or even 20 years down the road. We make plans, set goals, and daily strive to achieve how we imagine what we think our lives could be like if we just keep working towards that mental image. But, how often do you ever imagine yourself accomplishing all those things and then looking back and asking yourself as a Christian, "what did I really accomplish?" or "what did my life really stand for in the span of all eternity?"

I don't know about you, but when I get to the end of my earthly life as a Christian, I know there is one thing that I definitely do not want to happen. That is, I do not want to look back over my life and see that I have accomplished all of these earthly goals that I set for myself, yet I did not personally win a single soul to the Kingdom of Heaven. I do not want to come to the realization that all of my earthly time was spent doing things that, in the span of all eternity, really mean nothing.

On the contrary, what I do want to happen as I near the end of my life, if God so allows me, is to be able to look back and see how God has so faithfully used me to win an enormous amount of people to the Kingdom of heaven; that what I spent my time on earth doing did matter for all eternity. And furthermore, that what I did with my time here on earth will continue winning souls long after I am gone. In only this do I feel like I would have a great sense of fulfillment and accomplishment.

I believe as Christians, most of us inherently want to live our lives in a way that would be representative of the idea that when we get to the end of our lives we could reflect back and see how we spent our time reaching others for Jesus. We could see how we spent our time engaged in the Great Commission and doing what God had called us to do in reaching others. However, we must realize that this just does not happen automatically. I believe we must make conscious and physical efforts, through our thoughts and actions, in our daily lives to achieve this. Many of us are constantly setting goals and working to achieve earthly things such as a career, house, car, retirement, etc. when, as a Christian, we should be focused on setting and working towards a Soul Goal. We should be working towards a goal of a specific number of souls to reach in our lifetime with the message of the Gospel. This is the vital KEY to ensuring your success in accomplishing God's plan for your life on earth and for you to be able to one day look back and see the great work God has done through you that will last for all eternity.

What is Enough for You?

Using this concept, take a few moments to evaluate where you stand. Pretend you have fast-forwarded to the end of your life. You only have a few hours left to live. I want you to envision yourself feeling a great sense of accomplishment and a life well-lived because you know you have made a difference in the lives of so many people by sharing the Gospel with them. You know that because of you, many people have a living relationship with God and you will one day see them in heaven. Imagine that you had set a goal for the number of souls you wanted to reach with the Gospel and you know that with God's help, you far exceeded it. I want you to imagine how you may feel if this really was your life.

Now, after you have spent a few minutes imagining and visualizing this idea in your mind, begin to think about your current life now. What does it look like? What do you do on a daily, weekly, monthly basis? Think about your life over the past six months or year. What did you do? I want you to take a serious, hard look at evaluating your current life actions. The question is this: If you were to continue living the rest of your life exactly how you have been living over the past several months or even year, would it add up to the picture you just spent several minutes envisioning? Would the way you currently live your life, in the end, result in a life lived that had a massive impact in bringing a multitude of souls to heaven? Or, after thinking about it, what you spend most of your time doing now really wouldn't add up to much in the end?

I believe if you really take this simple exercise seriously, it can help you identify things in your life now that actually steal time away from you doing other things that really do matter. What things matter? Simple things like spending a little extra time with people and trying to make a difference in others' lives for Jesus.

Listen, if your current life actions don't add up to you making a significant impact in the lives of others throughout your lifetime, like you envisioned moments ago, at least now you know. You can now begin to make some positive changes in your life to ensure that when you get to the end, and look back, you'll truly feel a great sense of accomplishment. It would not be because of all the material "stuff" you accumulated, but rather because of all the lives you touched. I believe a good way to start steering your life in that direction today, is by setting a Soul Goal that you will continue to work towards from now until then!

To further understand what it means to have a Soul Goal and why you may want to have one, let's examine how a Soul Goal pertains to what is found in the Holy Bible. After we take a look at some scripture, I will then go further into what it means to have a Soul Goal in Part 2 of this topic.

CHAPTER FOUR

How Does a Soul Goal Pertain to Scripture?

For God so loved the world that he gave his one and only Son, that whoever believes in him shall not perish but have eternal life. (John 3:16)

God loves the world. More specifically, God loves you, me, and everyone else in the world. So much so, that he sent his one and only Son, Jesus, to die on a cross to pay for the sins of the world, that we might accept him as Lord and Savior of our lives and therefore receive the gift of eternal life. What a beautiful thing, that God so loves us even though we don't deserve it, and furthermore, gives us our own free will to choose whether we will love Him back or not.
True love can never be forced. For if it is forced, it cannot be love. The best decision I have ever made in my life is the decision I made to love the Lord back. It is the goal of my soul. And I hope you can say the same too.

The Goal for Your Soul

One day an expert in the law stood up to test Him. "Teacher," he asked, "what must I do to inherit eternal life?" "What is written in the Law?" Jesus replied. "How do you read it?" He answered, "Love the Lord your God with all your heart and with all your soul and with all your strength and with all your mind and 'Love your neighbor as yourself.'" "You have answered correctly," Jesus said. (Luke 10:25- 28)

Do you have a personal goal for your soul? As a Christian, you have believed in your heart and confessed with your mouth that Jesus Christ is Lord. You have accepted the gift of God's grace, his son Jesus Christ dying on the cross for your sins. You have now been reconciled unto God and have a living relationship with Him. You are a child of God.

The goal you now have for your soul is that one day it (you) will be in heaven with the Lord. And because that is your personal goal, you choose to love the Lord with your very soul, with your strength, with your mind and your heart as well. Therefore, the goal every Christian has for their own soul is one in the same, or at least should be.

Making the decision to accept eternal salvation through Jesus Christ is the most important decision you or anyone else could make, or has made in life. Therefore, it is no surprise that Jesus tells us that in order to inherit eternal life, we must love the Lord with all of our heart, soul, strength, and mind. Love Him because he first loved us (1 John 4:19) and he showed it by willingly laying down his life on the cross for our eternal salvation (1 John 3:16). Furthermore, take notice of what the expert in the law said that Jesus confirmed was correct: that you must love your neighbor as yourself.

That makes total sense. After all, if you have come to the personal conclusion that the message of the Gospel is correct and it is the most important decision you have ever made in your life, it makes sense that you would love other people enough to want them to make the most important decision in their life to accept salvation and become a follower of Jesus Christ as well.

Knowing that the goal you have for your own soul is to one day be with the Lord in heaven, the question now becomes "do you have a goal for the number of other people's souls you would like to reach or win with the most important message they could ever hear – the message of the Gospel?"

What are We Supposed to be Doing?

So you are a Christian. You consider yourself to be a follower of Christ. The question is, what in the world are you supposed to be doing now? Once you have believed in your heart that God raised him from the dead and confessed with your mouth that Jesus Christ is Lord (Romans 10:9), is there something you should be doing now that you are a Christian, that you weren't doing before as a non-Christian?

The answer is YES.

Therefore, if anyone is in Christ, the new creation has come: The old has gone, the new is here! All this is from God, who reconciled us to himself through Christ and gave us the ministry of reconciliation: that God was reconciling the world to himself in Christ, not counting people's sins against them. And he has committed to us the message of reconciliation. We are therefore Christ's ambassadors, as though God were making his appeal through us.

(2 Corinthians 5:17-20, emphasis added)

You did not choose me, but I chose you and appointed you so that you might go and bear fruit—fruit that will last—and so that whatever you ask in my name the Father will give you. (John 15:14-16)

Now that you are a Christian, consider yourself an ambassador for Christ with a very specific message to tell others: the message of reconciliation. God has committed to you the awesome responsibility to tell others the Good News message of Jesus Christ and how they can receive forgiveness of their sins by the grace of God. Simply put, you have a job to do. I believe having a Soul Goal will enable you to be organized, focused and strategic in making the most of your time and resources in accomplishing the ministry that God has committed to you. From now on, do not wonder if you are supposed to be doing something as a Christian, rather be very clear on the mission God has given you to reach others with the most important message in the world, the message of the Gospel.

The Great Commission

Then the eleven disciples went to Galilee, to the mountain where Jesus had told them to go. When they saw him, they worshiped him; but some doubted. Then Jesus came to them and said, "All authority in heaven and on earth has been given to me. Therefore go and make disciples of all nations, baptizing them in the name of the Father and of the Son and of the Holy Spirit, and teaching them to obey everything I have commanded you. And surely I am with you always, to the very end of the age." (Matthew 28:16-20)

This passage of scripture is known as the Great Commission. And what a mission it truly is. From Christ's death and resurrection, until this very day, it continues to be the single greatest mission on the face of the earth. In fact, the most renowned people in all of history who have made a significant impact in the world in reaching and winning others for the Kingdom of God all had this same mission at the very core of their life's work. The mission to go and make disciples, and the promise he will be with us as we go.

What an awesome thought to think that at the very moment you accepted Jesus Christ as your personal Lord and Savior, he commissioned you and trusted you with reaching others with the greatest message in the world. The message that can literally change the course of another's eternal destiny has been given to you. It has been entrusted to you. The question is, will you choose to embrace it and take action as God trusts you to do, or will you sit on the sidelines of your new life in Christ? Whether you will be successful or not in the Great Commission God has given you, is up to no-one else but you. Set a Soul Goal for the mission you have been given and start telling the world about Jesus.

Are You Qualified?

It is not that we think we are qualified to do anything on our own. Our qualification comes from God. He has enabled us to be ministers of his new covenant. This is a covenant not of written laws, but of the Spirit. The old written covenant ends in death; but under the new covenant, the Spirit gives life.

(2 Corinthians 3:5-6 NLT)

Are you qualified to share the message of the Gospel with others? Often times Christians don't share the message of the Gospel with others simply because they do not feel they are qualified to do so. Therefore, they convince themselves that it is someone else's job or responsibility that is better qualified than them, perhaps their pastor, to reach others with God's message of salvation. I believe that much of the time this thought or feeling is rooted in having a great reverence for what the Gospel is, the most important and powerful message on the face of the earth. And while it is true, it is the most important and powerful message someone could ever hear, every single Christian is not only qualified to tell it, they are commanded to do so in the Bible.

Realize that even though someone else, such as your pastor, may have more scripture memorized or may seem to have more knowledge of the scripture than you do, it does not disqualify you from your personal responsibility as a Christian to reach others with the message of the Gospel. God qualifying and trusting you, personally, with his message of salvation to tell others about is one of the most amazing, awesome, yet humbling aspects of his entire plan to save others.

Understand that in your own might you are not qualified to take part in reaching others with the Gospel. However, your qualification is not in your own might. Your qualification comes from God. It is he who has given you this mission and it is he who qualifies you and enables you to be successful in the mission if you, by your own free will, take action.

Remember, no matter how much scripture you know (or do not know), your personal relationship with the Lord and your personal testimony of salvation is unique to you and powerfully effective in reaching others when you share it. Keep in mind that not only are you qualified by God to share his message of salvation with others, but that he actually commanded you to do so. Setting a Soul Goal and dedicating your life working to reach it, is a great way to allow God to use you in what he has commanded, and qualified you, to do.

Holy Spirit – Your Helper

So now you understand that God has given you a mission, the Great Commission, and qualified you to do it. However, he doesn't stop there. He has furthermore given you the Holy Spirit to help and empower you in this mission.

I will ask the Father, and he will give you another advocate to help you and be with you forever— the Spirit of truth. (John 14:16-17)

But you will receive power when the Holy Spirit comes on you; and you will be my witnesses in Jerusalem, and in all Judea and Samaria, and to the ends of the earth." (Acts 1:8)

Aren't you glad God didn't set you up for failure by giving you an impossible mission and telling you to go do it on your own? Actually, if you really think about it, he did quite the opposite. He set you up to be hugely successful beyond your wildest dreams! He qualified you to do a mission you would never be qualified to do on your own. He entrusted you with it, and then gave you The Holy Spirit to empower and help you do what you would never be able to do in your own power and might. However, no matter how perfectly God has set you up for the most successful Christian life in reaching and winning others for the Kingdom of God, if you never seize the opportunity God has given you and take action in the mission, you will never fully realize the blessings and success in store for you. Choose to fully embrace the guidance, direction, and empowerment of the Holy Spirit in your life, as you seek to do the will of your Heavenly father and the mission he has given you, along with the Holy Spirit to help you accomplish it.

No One is Useless

There is no such thing as a useless part in the body of Christ. The Bible very clearly states that each and every one of us, as a Christian, has a specific part to fulfill as a member of the body of Christ.

Just as a body, though one, has many parts, but all its many parts form one body, so it is with Christ. For we were all baptized by one Spirit so as to form one body (1 Corinthians 12:12-13)

Know today, that if you are a Christian, whatever part you are in the body of Christ, it is an important one. For no single one part is insignificant. Furthermore, it is important that you function well in whatever part you have. As a Doctor, I know that some of the smallest, seemingly most insignificant parts of the human body, if not functioning well can cause the whole entire body to not function well at all. I encourage you to be the best you can be in allowing God to use you in whatever way he has for you. In doing so, I believe it will enable you to reach others with the message of the Gospel like never before.

Everyone Has Their Part

The eye can never say to the hand, "I don't need you." The head can't say to the feet, "I don't need you." In fact, some parts of the body that seem weakest and least important are actually the most necessary. And the parts we regard as less honorable are those we clothe with the greatest care. So we carefully protect those parts that should not be seen, while the more honorable parts do not require this special care. So God has put the body together such that extra honor and care are given to those parts that have less dignity. This makes for harmony among the members, so that all the members care for each other. If one part suffers, all the parts suffer with it, and if one part is honored, all the parts are glad. All of you together are Christ's body, and each of you is a part of it.
(1 Corinthians 12:21-27 NLT)

We all need each other. We all have a part. I have a part. You have a part. I must ask myself if I am doing my part. And you must ask yourself if you are doing your part too. Understand that in order for you to effectively do your part well; you must know specifically what your part is. Although this seems quite simple and obvious, a major reason some Christians fail to reach others with the message of the Gospel effectively is because they fail to specifically recognize what their part is in the body of Christ. You have a unique role in the body of Christ and correctly identifying your role is vital to your success in the mission God has given you to reach others with the message of salvation through Jesus Christ. Seek God's help in identifying what part you are in the body of Christ and implement your own personal Soul Goal to ensure whatever part you play is utilized to its' maximum potential. You may already know exactly what your part is, in this case if you don't already have one, consider using a Soul Goal to make you more efficient and effective in your part. A hint to knowing what your part is: identify the unique gifts and talents God has given you!

Hiding Your Gifts

Each of you should use whatever gift you have received to serve others, as faithful stewards of God's grace in its various forms. (1 Peter 4:10)

God has given each and every one of us specific and unique talents and gifts. I believe he has given them specifically to each one of us so that we would use them in reaching others with the Gospel. The unique talents and gifts God has given you are to be used to complete the purpose and mission God has for your life. The question is, are you using your unique gifts and talents to reach others, perhaps in only a way that you could reach them?

When working towards accomplishing your Soul Goal, identify the specific gifts and talents God has given you and use them to reach others. Remember, even though God has given this mission to all of us as Christians, he has given you unique gifts and talents that will enable you to reach others in a way that is specific to you. Don't make the mistake of hiding your God-given gifts and talents from others. Also, don't try to imitate someone else's gifts and talents if you are not gifted in that area as well. Simply be you. Identify your own unique gifts and talents and allow God to use you in a unique way to reach others as you pursue your own unique Soul Goal. Simply put, your unique God-given gifts and talents were meant to win souls.

You Were Designed to Bear Fruit

You were designed to bear fruit. Not only did God design you to bear fruit, but it pleases Him when you do. Additionally, as you commit yourself to telling others about Jesus and begin taking action in doing so, you will find yourself growing in the knowledge of God as God uses you to bear fruit (souls) that is pleasing to him. You will see Him work through you to touch other people's lives in ways you would have never even thought possible before.

We continually ask God to fill you with the knowledge of his will through all the wisdom and understanding that the Spirit gives, so that you may live a life worthy of the Lord and please him in every way: bearing fruit in every good work, growing in the knowledge of God (Colossians 1:9-10)

Have the mindset about yourself, and the internal determination, to be used by God to bear much fruit. I think the Apostle Paul reflects this attitude quite well when he writes; *I eagerly expect and hope that I will in no way be ashamed, but will have sufficient courage so that now as always Christ will be exalted in my body, whether by life or by death. For to me, to live is Christ and to die is gain. If I am to go on living in the body, this will mean fruitful labor for me.* (Philippians 1:20-22, emphasis added)

Honestly answer this question for yourself... Are you bearing much fruit? I believe having a Soul Goal will help you keep this kind of attitude towards fruitful labor at the forefront of your mind. You have probably heard the phrase before, "out of sight, out of mind" – do not let this become you. Instead, create a Soul Goal and by reflecting on it often, it will help ensure that your mind stays focused on what is important and pleasing to God: fruitful labor for the Kingdom of Heaven.

Closet Christian

You were never intended to be a "closet Christian," someone ashamed of, and concealing, their identity as a Christian. In fact, the very mission you have been given to reach others goes directly against the idea of concealing your Christian identity to those around you.

For I am not ashamed of the gospel, because it is the power of God that brings salvation to everyone who believes (Romans 1:16)

"Whoever acknowledges me before others, I will also acknowledge before my Father in heaven. But whoever disowns me before others, I will disown before my Father in heaven. (Matthew 10:32-33)

Ask yourself this question:

If I was taken to court, accused for being a Christian and witnessing to others, would there be overwhelming evidence to convict me?

I believe having a Soul Goal can help you overcome the enemy's attacks in trying to keep you silent or feeling ashamed of the Gospel. Any time you find yourself at a crossroads between speaking up and witnessing, versus staying silent, think about your Soul Goal and take action. When you do so, the result of speaking up in this opportunity just may result in you becoming one more person closer to reaching your Soul Goal.

You are meant to be a shining light...

Let Your Light Shine Bright

"You are the light of the world. A town built on a hill cannot be hidden. Neither do people light a lamp and put it under a bowl. Instead they put it on its stand, and it gives light to everyone in the house. In the same way, let your light shine before others, that they may see your good deeds and glorify your Father in heaven." (Matthew 5:14-16)

Light allows people to see. One way you can allow your light to shine is by telling others what God has done and is doing in your life. Tell them your personal testimonies. Be a witness to the living God being alive in your life, not to glorify yourself, but rather that your Father in heaven is glorified in and through your testimony. On the contrary, one way to hide your light so that no one even knows you are a Christian is by staying silent. If you see someone in the dark and you refuse to turn the light on, how do you expect them to see?

How, then, can they call on the one they have not believed in? And how can they believe in the one of whom they have not heard? And how can they hear without someone preaching to them? And how can anyone preach unless they are sent? As it is written: "How beautiful are the feet of those who bring good news!" (Romans 10:14-15)

Choose to be a shining light by speaking up. Make it a point to include speaking to others about Jesus in your daily and weekly objectives toward reaching your Soul Goal.

"Anyone who welcomes you welcomes me, and anyone who welcomes me welcomes the one who sent me." (Matthew 10:40)

When you let your light shine by sharing your personal testimonies, those who receive you and your testimonies about God, are allowing themselves to receive from God. YOU become the conduit by which people receive from God.

World's Approach vs. Soul Goal Minded Approach

Don't copy the behavior and customs of this world, but let God transform you into a new person by changing the way you think. Then you will learn to know God's will for you, which is good and pleasing and perfect. (Romans 12:2 NLT)

As a Christian, you must be careful to not copy the behavior and customs of this world. I believe this can be applied to setting goals as well. It is not difficult to see that the goals non-Christians strive to achieve are often common representations of behaviors and customs of this world, driven by the desire of self-fulfillment without giving any thought to eternal value and/or significance. As a follower of Jesus Christ, you must not fall into the same trap of only thinking about goals in reference to your time here on earth; rather, you must consider setting goals and taking actions towards those goals in terms of what they mean for all eternity. In doing this, you change the way you think by *setting your mind on things above, and not on earthly things below* (Colossians 3:2). Recognize, as a Christian, that the way you think should be quite different from someone who is not a Christian. Know that it is God's will for you to tell others about Jesus, for this is pleasing unto Him.

Mind of Christ

Whoever claims to live in him must live as Jesus did. (1 John 2:6)

So prepare your minds for action and exercise self-control. Put all your hope in the gracious salvation that will come to you when Jesus Christ is revealed to the world. So you must live as God's obedient children. Don't slip back into your old ways of living to satisfy your own desires. You didn't know any better then. But now you must be holy in everything you do, just as God who chose you is holy. For the Scriptures say, "You must be holy because I am holy."

(1 Peter 1:13-16 NLT)

What does it truly mean to have the mind of Christ? Although I do not know every thought that went through Jesus' mind while he was here on earth, there is one thought I know he was thinking about all of the time... the thought about saving souls. The recordings of Jesus' words and actions found in the Bible show us quite clearly that this one thought saturated his mind continuously. It was his very life's mission, even unto death. Notice how Jesus was determined to reach his goal even knowing Herod was out to kill him.

At that time some Pharisees came to Jesus and said to him, "Leave this place and go somewhere else. Herod wants to kill you." He replied, "Go tell that fox, 'I will keep on driving out demons and healing people today and tomorrow, and on the third day I will reach my goal.' (Luke 13:31-32)

As a follower of Jesus Christ, how often do you think about saving souls? How often do you have the mind of Christ in this area when it comes to everyday life? I am convinced that the more we think about saving the lost, the more we will actually take actions to do it. When you set a Soul Goal and begin to work towards reaching it, naturally it will most likely cause you to think about reaching the lost more than you would without having a specific goal for souls.

"For the Son of Man came to seek and to save the lost." (Luke 19:10)

The Greatest Goal and Accomplishment

Do you realize if you have a Soul Goal, you could literally have a goal that is far greater than any goal of even the wealthiest, most successful person on the face of the earth if they don't have a Soul Goal themselves? There have been multitudes of people who have spent their whole entire lives striving to achieve goal after goal in order to amass great wealth, and have even been successful doing it, just to find out in the end, they are still empty inside and they cannot take any of their wealth with them. The Bible puts it this way... *What good is it for someone to gain the whole world, and yet lose or forfeit their very self?* (Luke 9:25) Unfortunately, this has happened to many people. The Bible says, *he that winneth souls is wise* (Proverbs 11:30 KJV). Be wise. Forget about setting goals to try to gain the whole world. Set a Soul Goal and focus on winning souls. *But seek first his kingdom and his righteousness, and all these things will be given to you as well* (Matthew 6:33).

Setting Captives Free

"The Spirit of the Lord is upon me, for he has anointed me to bring Good News to the poor. He has sent me to proclaim that captives will be released, that the blind will see, that the oppressed will be set free, and that the time of the Lord's favor has come." (Luke 4:18-19 NLT)

So if the Son sets you free, you will be free indeed. (John 8:36)

Jesus came to set the captives free. It is the message of the Gospel. But, who are the captives and what has them bound? Simply put, the captives are every single person who has never accepted the saving grace message of reconciliation unto God through Jesus Christ and therefore is still bound by sin and death. Having a Soul Goal means having a goal to break people out of the chains of sin and death that has them bound. In other words, you can think of your Soul Goal in the terms of how many people do I want God to use me to break free from the bondages of sin and death and into an eternal life with Jesus? What an awesome goal to have in life!

Make it Your Goal to Please Him

So we make it our goal to please him, whether we are at home in the body or away from it. For we must all appear before the judgment seat of Christ, so that each of us may receive what is due us for the things done while in the body, whether good or bad. (2 Corinthians 5:9-10, emphasis added)

And he died for all, that those who live should no longer live for themselves but for him who died for them and was raised again. (2 Corinthians 5:15)

I believe telling others about Jesus and how they can receive salvation and furthermore, how to have a living relationship with the Lord, pleases Him. Having a Soul Goal and working towards accomplishing it, is one way you can actually set a goal to please the Lord.

Eternal Life Living

Take hold of the eternal life to which you were called when you made your good confession in the presence of many witnesses. (1 Timothy 6:12)

After you receive salvation through Jesus Christ, you should no longer live making decisions and taking actions only based on your earthly existence. As a Christian, the way you live and the decisions you make should be made in consideration of the consequences not only for your life here on earth, but more importantly for your life throughout all eternity. In other words, as much as possible, no longer make decisions based on your fleeting moments of life on earth, but rather make decisions based on what the consequences of those decisions will be for all eternity.

When thinking about just how long eternity is, we come to the realization that our earthly existence is but a brief moment in time. However, ironically it is how we spend this short amount of time that determines how we will live for the rest of all eternity.

Dear friends, I warn you as "temporary residents and foreigners" to keep away from worldly desires that wage war against your very souls.

(1 Peter 2:11 NLT)

So many people believe in Jesus Christ to save them from their sins so that they can spend eternity with God, yet they continue living on earth as if their earthly life is the only life they are ever going to have. As Christian's, we must be careful to not make the mistake of living only with our earthly life in mind. Rather, keep your mind set on heaven and eternity as you go through this life on earth.

Make decisions today, tomorrow, and for the rest of your earthly life based off of what those decisions mean for all eternity. For example, make it a point to give to the church, to missions, and to special offerings; serve in areas of ministry through your local church, tell others about Jesus, raise your children in a Christian home, etc. Try to be intentional in doing these things because you not only recognize their significance for your life on earth, but also because you value their impact for all eternity. In many ways, the benefits of having a Soul Goal can be measured in terms of both earthly and internal impact. The earthly lives of those you reach can be transformed for the rest of their lives as they develop their own personal relationship with the Lord. In addition, it changes their eternal destination as well. Having a Soul Goal benefits both them and you, now and for all eternity.

CHAPTER FIVE

What it Means to Have a Soul Goal
Part 2

In an effort to fully understand what a Soul Goal is and how it fits within the parameters of your life as a Christian, think about the following terms and the differences between them for a few minutes:

Vision – Describes what you would like to become or how you see yourself in the future. As a Christian, you must have a vision. *Where there is no vision, the people perish* (Proverbs 29:18 KJV) Furthermore, I believe you should get a vision of yourself that goes beyond your earthly existence and perhaps reflects how you would like to see yourself standing before the Lord one day.

Consider the sample Question and Answer below. These may help you understand a vision for your life as a Christian:

Question: How would you like to present yourself to the Lord once your earthly life is finished?

Your answer: As a living sacrifice who spent my time on earth doing the will of the Father, which includes telling others and making disciples to the best of my God-given ability.

Therefore, I urge you, brothers and sisters, in view of God's mercy, to offer your bodies as a living sacrifice, holy and pleasing to God—this is your true and proper worship. Do not conform to the pattern of this world, but be transformed by the renewing of your mind. Then you will be able to test and approve what God's will is—his good, pleasing and perfect will. (Romans 12:1-2)

It is the pursuit of a vision like this that should motivate you in your daily life. I believe as Christians, we should have a common vision of what our lives should look like on that day. Why? Because we all share in the same mission… The Great Commission.

I don't know about you, but one day I hope to stand before the Lord and hear the words *"Well done, good and faithful servant."* (Matthew 25:21) I do not want to hear this because I am better than anyone else, but rather because of how I *took up my cross daily* (Luke 9:23) and lived my life on earth trying to do my best to fulfill God's plan and purpose for my life. Meaning, a purpose to reach others with the message of salvation and reconciliation unto God. I believe creating and working towards a Soul Goal can be an effective way to stay focused on our vision as Christians and one day experiencing that vision become a reality.

Here is great question to ask yourself to see if your current vision for your life lines up with the vision I described above:

If I were to achieve all the strategic goals I currently have in my life from now until the end of my earthly life, do I think it would amount to hearing God say, "well done thou good and faithful servant"? If not, you may seriously want to consider implementing a personal Soul Goal into your life as soon as possible.

Mission – Describes what you are now and your reason for existence. Simply put, you could say your mission as a Christian is this… I am a Christian (describes what you are) and I follow and serve the Lord all the days of my life (describes your reason for existence). Since as a Christian you have *died to yourself and are now alive in Christ* (Galatians 2:20), you take on the mission of Christ in reaching others with the message of salvation; and, furthermore making disciples. This is your Great CoMission in life as a Christian.

Therefore, since Christ suffered in his body, arm yourselves also with the same attitude, because whoever suffers in the body is done with sin. As a result, they do not live the rest of their earthly lives for evil human desires, but rather for the will of God. (1 Peter 4:1-2)

Goal – A specific target you intend to reach in the long-term. As a Christian, you could say your Soul Goal is the specific number of souls you hope to reach or win for the Kingdom of God by the end of your earthly life.

Soul Goal – a specific number of souls you intend to reach or win in the long run.

Think of it this way… You set a goal because you are on a mission to reach a specific vision.

In other words, as a Christian you set a Soul Goal because you are on the Great Commission to reach others with the message of salvation because you have the vision to one day stand before the Lord and hear Him say: *"Well done, good and faithful servant."* (Matthew 25:21)

If you have a lifelong Soul Goal, it furthermore makes sense to set smaller objectives to help keep you on track towards accomplishing your goal. Therefore…

Objectives – Are exact steps that you identify you must take to help you reach your goal. They are designed to produce specific results within a specific amount of time. They clearly state what is to be achieved, how it is to be achieved, who is going to achieve it, and when it is to be achieved by. Think short-term deadlines and steps that must be taken to reach the deadlines. Objectives are easily measureable and are therefore, great indicators to how well you are doing towards reaching your overall goal.

I will cover objectives and how you can incorporate them into a Soul Goal later in this book. For now, just understand there is a difference between Vision, Mission, Goals and Objectives, and even though they are each distinctly different, they all synergistically work together.

Why Do People Set Goals?

Now that you have a basic overview of the differences between Vision, Mission, Goals, and Objectives, let's take a deeper look at setting goals. Why do people set goals? Why do you set goals?

While there may be many different motivations for setting goals, I believe the strategy of setting goals boils down to one fundamental purpose. Setting goals help people accomplish things they either need, should, or want to accomplish. Simply put, when you set a goal to accomplish something, you are much more likely to take action toward that goal and furthermore, much more likely to actually accomplish it. Therefore, by using the strategy of setting goals in our lives, we are intending to set ourselves up for success.

Goals give us a destination to work towards. And since we have identified a destination that we would like to reach, we can then begin to clearly identify action steps we need to take towards the goal and start taking them.

For example, I used to think running a marathon was unreachable for me. After all, a marathon is 26.2 miles long and I could barely run a half of a mile without feeling like I was going to die. However, once I decided that running a complete marathon was a goal that I wanted to achieve, I could then begin to clearly identify the actions I would need to take to eventually reach my goal. I came up with a training schedule that outlined exactly how often, and how far I would need to run every day for several months to eventually work my way up to being able to run 26.2 miles.

As you can imagine, there were days that were extremely uncomfortable where I didn't want to run at all, and other days where I felt a great sense of accomplishment. There were many ups and downs along the way, but because I had set a goal and identified the steps I needed to take to accomplish it, even on the worst days I was able to push myself beyond any thoughts of giving up. Eventually I accomplished my goal and completed the Chicago Marathon. However, I didn't stop there. I then went on to complete the New York City Marathon in an even faster time than I ran the Chicago Marathon. Looking back, I had gone from barely being able to run a half mile, to now running, not one, but two full marathons. That's what goals do. They give you a destination to work towards and a determination to reach it that perhaps, you wouldn't have if you never set the goal in the first place.

You see, I believe as a Christian you can set a goal for a specific number of souls you want to reach or win with the message of the Gospel throughout your lifetime. I call it a Soul Goal. And once you set it, you can then begin to clearly identify steps you should take to reach your goal. I can assure you that in life you will have your ups and downs, moments of great triumph and moments of great despair. However, through it all, if you keep your eyes and your actions set on the eternal goal of reaching and winning souls, you can be sure that what you will accomplish will far exceed your current limited understanding of what God's full potential for your life actually is.

Soul Winning Lifestyle

Make soul winning your lifestyle. Soul winning should not just be something you do every once in a while, it should become a way of life for you. It should be a lifestyle you condition your mind to think about and actions to live out every single day of your life.

One particular Sunday I was a guest speaker at a church. I had been asked to speak about missions. Although I believe the pastor and the missions department who invited me were expecting me to specifically talk about my experiences in doing missions abroad in other countries, when I began to prepare my message, I felt the Lord urging me to particularly talk about the Great CoMission that each and every Christian is called to live out in our daily lives. Specifically, that being on a mission does not start when we set foot on foreign soil after taking an airplane ride to another land. Instead, being on a mission is who we are as Christians every single day of our lives.

After I delivered the message, I was standing out in the hallway of the church. A man approached me with tears in his eyes. He began to explain to me that he had always wanted to go on a mission trip to another country. He had been going to church most of his life, but whenever the opportunity arose to go on an overseas mission trip, a life situation would happen that prevented him from going.

He then started telling me that when I was talking about how we, as Christians, are to consider ourselves as living everyday as if we were on one big, long continuous mission trip, that even if you were to go on a mission trip overseas, really that mission trip would just be an extension of what you already should be doing in your everyday life. He said in that moment, it was as if a huge light bulb suddenly went on in his mind.

For the first time, he got it. All this time he had the desire to see souls saved, yet for some reason in his mind, he thought he had to physically get on an airplane and go somewhere else and then the mission would start. He began to explain that due to the nature of his job, he often has people come to him for help that are stranded from out-of-state. He said, looking back over the years, it was as if God had strategically placed him in these situations so he could speak into other peoples' lives as he helped them with their need. He could see that despite having never been on a mission trip before, God had used him in a way to perhaps reach others. He said the difference between then, and now going forward is, that "now I am going to intentionally tell them about Jesus. I now know my mission field is not some foreign land, but rather where I go to work every single day."

Wow! What a powerful testimony! I think it is safe to say that he was more excited to go to work the next day than what he had probably been in a long time. I believe we can make soul winning a lifestyle by which we live by. Whatever situation, job, or position in life you find yourself in, approach your days as if you were on a mission field. You may just come to see that situation or job you currently find yourself in, is the exact place that God has positioned you to reach someone around you.

A word of encouragement... lifestyles typically do not change overnight. They can, but more often than not, changing your lifestyle is going to be a process you go through over a period of time. That is another good reason for you to adopt a Soul Goal. Having a Soul Goal will help you to stay focused in developing a soul winning lifestyle over an extended period of time. Eventually, soul winning will become "second nature" to you. It is not necessarily about where you find yourself now, as much as it is about which direction are you heading in. Are you heading in a lifestyle direction that produces fruit for the Kingdom, or not? Only you can answer that question. Consider setting a Soul Goal in an effort to produce maximum fruit for the Kingdom of God.

A KEY To Lifestyle...

My hope for you, is that eventually in everything you do, you can see how it may be connected to your Soul Goal in some way. Hopefully your Soul Goal becomes not only a goal, but a core principle in your life by which you intentionally develop your lifestyle around.

When you look at Jesus' life and ministry described in the Bible, you can see that he made reaching souls the center of his lifestyle. Everything else he did in life revolved around winning souls. As followers of Jesus Christ, knowing the mission to reach people has now been given to us, I believe we should develop our lifestyle around this core mission as well.

Understand, there is a huge difference between trying to fit God and the mission he has given you into your lifestyle and how you want to live, versus placing God first in your life and developing your lifestyle and how you live around his mission and calling for your life. One seeks to fit Him, and the mission, into a lifestyle that is driven by self-fulfilling desires and personal preferences. The other seeks to develop a lifestyle that is going to be most conducive to producing fruit (harvest of souls) for the Kingdom of God, no matter how desirable or preferential it may be.

The key is this... Commit to winning souls, create a Soul Goal, and develop your lifestyle around purposely and intentionally doing things that will open the doors of opportunity for you to work towards reaching your Soul Goal.

Mission Trip

Did you ever think about why Christians get so fired up about going on a Missions trip and reaching people with the Gospel more than they do in their daily lives? As Christians, the mission to reach people with the Gospel and the willingness for us to take action in doing it, should be just as alive in us whether we are on a Missions trip or at home going about our daily lives.

The fact of the matter is though; many Christians spend much of their time in their daily lives not active in the mission. Why? I believe there are many reasons why this is true in the lives of many Christians, however, many of those reasons boil down to one simple point: they simply don't think about it. Their minds are consumed by so many other things, including the worries of this life, that they rarely think about making it a goal to share Jesus with others.

"Therefore I tell you, do not worry about your life, what you will eat or drink; or about your body, what you will wear. Is not life more than food, and the body more than clothes? (Matthew 6:25)

Furthermore...

For the pagans run after all these things, and your heavenly Father knows that you need them. But seek first his kingdom and his righteousness, and all these things will be given to you as well. (Matthew 6:32-33)

So why is it then, that when a Christian goes on a Missions trip, all of a sudden, the Christian who hasn't told a single soul about Jesus in the last year, gets so excited to tell others about Jesus? I believe, in part, it has to do with the same reason why people go on vacations with the idea that they are going to spend a week or two relaxing and not thinking about anything else other than laying around on the beach sipping piña coladas. The point is, they stop worrying about all the other cares of this life for a short moment in time.

By no means am I saying a Missions trip is a vacation, because often times, Christians work more on a Missions trip than they do back home. However, the point I am trying to make is this, I believe a big reason why Christians get so fired up about telling others about Jesus on a Missions trip more than they do in their daily lives is because, for a brief moment in time they stop thinking about all the worries of this life and begin to focus on their true mission in life as a Christian to reach others for the Kingdom of God.

It's true, many Christians go on Missions trips and see God do some incredible things that they had never experienced back home. Why is that? I believe one of the reasons is, is that they are not active in the mission when they are back home. Because they are now on a Missions trip, they are constantly living every moment of their time focused on the mission at hand. Therefore, God shows up in a mighty way to help them in their mission. However, if the same Christians would live with the same focus and mindset everyday back home that they have on the mission field, I believe they would see

God use them to touch the lives of people all the time in their everyday lives.

Realize that whether you are on a "Missions trip" in a foreign land or you are simply at home going about your daily life activities, you are on a mission. Therefore, give your worries to God and fill your mind with the thoughts of Heaven, staying focused on the mission at hand. Make a conscious effort to keep the same level of enthusiasm you would have on a Missions trip to reach others, the same level of enthusiasm you have in your daily life. Setting your mind on your Soul Goal and objectives will help keep the flame burning deep inside of you and your light shining bright to those around you.

For this reason I remind you to fan into flame the gift of God, which is in you through the laying on of my hands. For the Spirit God gave us does not make us timid, but gives us power, love and self-discipline. So do not be ashamed of the testimony about our Lord or of me his prisoner. Rather, join with me in suffering for the gospel, by the power of God. He has saved us and called us to a holy life—not because of anything we have done but because of his own purpose and grace. (2 Timothy 1:6-9)

How Many People Through You?

Self-Evaluation. Ask yourself these two questions:
1. How many people have you personally seen saved by Jesus through you?
2. How often do you talk about or communicate God's power to save or heal others?

Jesus now works through you. You are the vessel by which salvation flows through to others.

How, then, can they call on the one they have not believed in? And how can they believe in the one of whom they have not heard? And how can they hear without someone preaching to them? And how can anyone preach unless they are sent? As it is written: "How beautiful are the feet of those who bring good news!"
(Romans 10:14-15)

It works like this: if you are never communicating God's ability to forgive sins, God's ability to meet needs, God's love for every single human being, than you will most likely never see people saved through you. You may live your whole life as a believer, but never see a single soul saved through you.

The amount of time you spend communicating God's love to others, whether it's God's ability to heal or to save, correlates to how often you will see God's power do such acts through you. If you never communicate God to others, you will never see God being received by others, through you.

It's just that simple.

CHAPTER SIX

Why Would a Christian Want to Set a Soul Goal?

"Christianity, if false, is of no importance, and if true, of infinite importance. The only thing it cannot be is moderately important." - C. S. Lewis

If the Gospel is not true, it is of no importance and all the other things in your life should be valued more important than a false religion. However, if it is true, it should be valued by you as (in the words of C. S. Lewis) an infinite importance. My friend, if you are a Christian, you have already come to the definitive conclusion that the Gospel found in the Bible is true. Therefore, everything in your life and belief system should be based off this fundamental truth and you should value your salvation as perhaps the most important truth by which you live your life by.

Additionally, as a Christian, we understand the importance and value placed on this message that was once shared with us by someone else. Similarly, we should place a high level of importance in sharing this message with others as well. If it is the most important message you have ever heard in your life, it is the most important message you could ever tell someone else.

Having a Soul Goal to tell others about the message of the Gospel, and see them receive salvation through Jesus Christ, is not simply a goal to tell others a message. Setting a Soul Goal is committing yourself to tell a certain number of people The Most Important Message they could ever hear, period. Now that is a goal worth having.

Best Earthly Time Investment

"Look, I am coming soon! My reward is with me, and I will give to each person according to what they have done." (Revelation 22:12)

I am sure you have heard the phrase "time is money." It is a phrase commonly used by many people, especially when it comes to a job or a profession. It is a worldly term and as Christians, we must be very careful to not just see the value of our time as measured by an earthly reward. We must remind ourselves that God can, and will reward us, with eternal rewards based on how we spend our time here on earth. In other words, as Christians, perhaps instead of saying "time is money," we should say "time is eternal rewards" to indicate that we understand how we spend our time isn't just valued by a certain amount of earthly money, but rather by a certain amount of eternal reward.

Have you ever thought about this… what are the things that Jesus will reward you for that you have done, or are doing? The fact of the matter is that you can only do so much with your time. In other words, your time is limited and how you choose to spend it will either amount to being eternally rewarded by God or not.

I tell you, open your eyes and look at the fields! They are ripe for harvest. Even now the one who reaps draws a wage and harvests a crop for eternal life (John 4:35-36)

In the secular world, you could spend countless hours going to seminars and workshops to learn how to make the best investments with your time, and many people do. However, the vast majority of these events are centered on how to make the best investment with your time in order to make the most money with your time. The focus never goes beyond thinking in terms of anything more than earthly wealth. While learning how to be most efficient with your time to make the most money in exchange for it is not all bad, as Christians we must not fall into the trap of only thinking about exchanging our time for money. We must think in terms of eternal impact.

For the love of money is a root of all kinds of evil. Some people, eager for money, have wandered from the faith and pierced themselves with many griefs.
(1 Peter 6:10)

Understand this: money itself is not bad. Having a lot of money is not bad either. It is how you use the money that determines whether it is good or bad. Learning and knowing how to earn the most money in exchange for your time is not necessarily a bad thing, as long as at the core of why you exchange your time for that money is, in part, because you ultimately have a plan for using that money to exchange it for eternal rewards.

How do you exchange earthly money for eternal rewards? Great question. Invest the money in Kingdom work being done on earth. One quite obvious way this can be done is by giving to missions, evangelism, and/or ministry work. The bottom line is this, the best investment you can make with your time on earth is telling others about Jesus and making disciples. Whether you are doing that directly yourself, or you are using the money you have earned in exchange for your time to do that, the reward you will receive for doing that is far more valuable than any earthly reward you could receive. Having a Soul Goal and spending your time towards achieving it will result in one of the best time investments you could ever make on earth, the eternal investment of saving souls.

Heavenly Treasure

"Do not store up for yourselves treasures on earth, where moths and vermin destroy, and where thieves break in and steal. But store up for yourselves treasures in heaven, where moths and vermin do not destroy, and where thieves do not break in and steal. For where your treasure is, there your heart will be also.
(Matthew 6:19-21)

Another benefit given to you, by God, for winning souls is heavenly treasure. Many people spend all of their time accumulating earthly treasure and spend no time, or even think about, storing up heavenly treasure. Have you noticed, whether Christian or not, people get very strategic about financial management and building earthly wealth, yet often times approach building heavenly wealth in a casual, haphazard, non-important, reckless, and careless way? I believe if Christians spent as much time carefully planning for, budgeting, and managing their eternal wealth as they did for their earthly wealth, we would see a level of evangelism happening across the earth like never before. In much of the same way as you would set a goal for your earthly finances, set a goal for building heavenly wealth by setting a Soul Goal. Then, take daily, weekly, and monthly action steps toward reaching that goal.

Re-Define Your Goals

The basic necessities of life, I get it. Food, water, shelter. However, as simple as that may seem, the reality is… living in the complex, industrialized and technological world of our time causes most of us to go far beyond our pursuit of the basic necessities of life. In doing so, we set earthly goals that are often a direct reflection of the world we find ourselves living in and our own personal idea of how we want to find ourselves living in it. Often times, we set these goals giving no thought to our eternal existence beyond our earthly experience. They are simply goals for the here and now.

Nonetheless, even though these goals are usually set giving no thought to their eternal significance in our lives, it is interesting to note, that I believe they are usually set in order to, hopefully, satisfy our own internal desire to live a worthwhile and fulfilling life.

However, once you become a Christian, you are immediately awakened to a new life. You now have a new mission in life to complete that you did not have before. The mission to tell others about the same saving grace you now have come to know and accept for yourself. The question is, where do you place this new mission God has given you in relationship to all the other goals and objectives you had previously set in your life? In other words, once you became a Christian, did you ever think about and prioritize the mission to reach others that God has given you in relationship to your other goals?

I believe once you become a Christian, you must do a little re-defining and re-structuring of goals and priorities in your mind and life. Why? Because the goals you once had and the priority in which you placed them were all done revolving around you. Now that you are a Christian, your life does not revolve around you; rather, it revolves around the Lord. Therefore, I believe at minimum, it is necessary to re-align your goals as a Christian with God's plan, purpose, and mission for your life. For some, re-aligning your goals may involve getting rid of, possibly even replacing, or re-prioritizing your old goals, but I believe this is a necessary process that we (you), as a Christian, must fully embrace. A fundamental step to renewing your mind to align with the will of God for your life is by making the reading of the Bible a normal, consistent, and regular occurrence in your life. Furthermore, I believe setting a Soul Goal will help you take practical steps that reflect your renewed mind, priorities and goals as a follower of Jesus Christ.

So practically speaking, what does that mean? Maybe before you were a Christian, you had goals for your family, career, retirement, house, money, car, education, etc. Whether you wrote them down or not, in your mind you placed a certain value or priority level on these goals. Now that you are a Christian, how do you re-align these old goals with the new priorities in your life?

I believe the answer can be found by asking yourself this one question: how do each of these goals fit within my God-given purpose and mission in life? I cannot answer this question for you, but I do believe I can point you in the right direction. Try to re-envision the goals you have in your life in a way that accomplishing them would help you reach your Soul Goal. In other words, how would accomplishing the goal for your family, career, retirement, house, money, car, education, etc. help you reach more people for the Kingdom of God?

When you begin to think like this, you may discover that some of the goals you had for different areas of your life are just not nearly as important as they once were to you. In addition, the more you are able to connect all the goals in your life to God's plan and purpose for your life, the less you will feel like you are trying to live being torn between two different sets of goals; your own personal goals, and the goals God has given you. As much as possible, try to understand how accomplishing the goals you have in your life will better enable you to live the life God has called you to live. A light shining in the darkness. A salt to the earth. A person with passion, on mission, with a divine purpose for living.

What Would You be Doing Differently?

By now you should be quite clear in understanding that the message of the Gospel has been committed to you to tell others about Jesus. As a Christian, there should be no question in your mind that you have a personal obligation and responsibility to tell others. Therefore, it makes sense that perhaps there are a certain number of souls you are responsible to reach with this message in your lifetime.

For the sake of looking at the power and significance of having a Soul Goal from a different perspective, let's just hypothetically pretend that in an instant, whether by revelation, dream, or vision, God showed you an exact number of people you were supposed to reach with the message of the Gospel throughout your lifetime. Let's imagine that you now know that throughout your lifetime, you are supposed to reach 1 million souls. Think about this for a moment. Try to visualize this in your mind as though it were reality.

While imagining that you were responsible to tell 1 million people about Jesus throughout your lifetime, take a few minutes and honestly ask yourself these questions;

- What would I be doing differently in my life that I am not doing right now?
- Would I have a different vision for what my life should look like from now until the end of my life?
- Would I be doing anything different with my time?
- Would I be reading my Bible more?
- Would I be praying more?
- Would I be working towards other goals that I currently have in my life as much as I am now?
- Would I be going to church more?
- Would I be speaking to more people about Jesus?

- Think of other questions to ask yourself in an effort to honestly evaluate your daily actions in reaching souls.

Even though this is a hypothetical example using a made-up number, taking the time to think about your awesome responsibility and obligation as a Christian in this way can give you a completely different perspective on life. If after asking yourself the previous questions you feel a sense that you may be falling behind in what God has for you, I want to encourage you to set a Soul Goal and start taking steps toward doing those things you feel are either missing in your life or you would be doing differently if you knew there were a certain number of people you were supposed to reach in your lifetime. That way, when you get further down the road of life you will be able to look back and see how your life has changed from now until then in being more effective in reaching others for the Kingdom of God.

Your Potential

Fact: If you are not actively engaged in the Great Commission, you are living less than your full potential in life as a Christian. Who knowingly wants to live less than their full potential in life? Not me. Walking in your full potential in life as a Christian, being everything God wants you to be, being everything you should want to be for God and yourself, requires you to be actively engaged in the Great Commission. Implementing a Soul Goal in your life and consistently completing objectives towards achieving it, helps you to maintain a systematic approach to walking in your full potential as a Christian.

Gathering or Scattering

Are you gathering or scattering?

"Whoever is not with me is against me, and whoever does not gather with me scatters." (Matthew 12:30)

Simply put, whether you realize it or not, you are influencing people every day. The question is, do your actions as a Christian influence people in the direction of Jesus or not? By having a Soul Goal and working towards objectives in your daily life to reach it, you become more consciously aware of taking specific actions to ensure you are gathering and not scattering. Otherwise, without a Soul Goal it is much easier to go through life without even thinking about taking specific actions toward reaching people or you may simply just go about your daily business never knowing whether or not your actions are actually making a positive difference in the lives of others for the Kingdom of God.

Four Categories of People

Again Jesus began to teach by the lake. The crowd that gathered around him was so large that he got into a boat and sat in it out on the lake, while all the people were along the shore at the water's edge. He taught them many things by parables, and in his teaching said: "Listen! A farmer went out to sow his seed. As he was scattering the seed, some fell along the path, and the birds came and ate it up. Some fell on rocky places, where it did not have much soil. It sprang up quickly, because the soil was shallow. But when the sun came up, the plants were scorched, and they withered because they had no root. Other seed fell among thorns, which grew up and choked the plants, so that they did not bear grain. Still other seed fell on good soil. It came up, grew and produced a crop, some multiplying thirty, some sixty, some a hundred times." (Mark 4:1-8)

Then Jesus said to them, "Don't you understand this parable? How then will you understand any parable? The farmer sows the word. Some people are like seed along the path, where the word is sown. As soon as they hear it, Satan comes and takes away the word that was sown in them. Others, like seed sown on rocky places, hear the word and at once receive it with joy. But since they have no root, they last only a short time. When trouble or persecution comes because of the word, they quickly fall away. Still others, like seed sown among thorns, hear the word; but the worries of this life, the deceitfulness of wealth and the desires for other things come in and choke the word, making it unfruitful. Others, like seed sown on good soil, hear the word, accept it, and produce a crop—some thirty, some sixty, some a hundred times what was sown." (Mark 4:13-20)

Notice in this passage of scripture there are four categories of people:

Category 1: Those who hear the Word, and the devil comes and takes the word away from them.

Category 2: Those who hear the Word, believe for a while, but as trouble comes or people persecute them, they fall away.

Category 3: Those who hear the Word, but are consumed by life's worries, riches, and pleasures.

Category 4: Those who hear the Word, accept it, and <u>produce a crop.</u>

The question is: what category would you say you are in? A good question to ask yourself is: "am I producing a crop?"

Determine to be a doer of the Word and not merely just a listener of the Word.

Do not merely listen to the word, and so deceive yourselves. Do what it says. Anyone who listens to the word but does not do what it says is like someone who looks at his face in a mirror and, after looking at himself, goes away and immediately forgets what he looks like. But whoever looks intently into the perfect law that gives freedom, and continues in it—not forgetting what they have heard, but doing it—they will be blessed in what they do. (James 1:22-25)

Serving God with a Clear Conscience

I thank God, whom I serve, as my ancestors did, with a clear conscience
(2 Timothy 1:3)

Understanding that you have a responsibility to serve God by spreading his message of reconciliation to the lost; can you honestly say that you are serving God with a clear conscience? Maybe you are serving God with an unclear conscience. Maybe you are not serving God at all. Whatever the case may be, it seems to me, that serving God with a clear conscience could only be achieved by intentionally and specifically doing what you know God wants you to do. On the contrary, knowingly not doing what you know God wants you to do will lead to you having an unclear conscience toward serving God. In other words, if you know God wants you to reach and disciple people, and you don't do it, is it possible to have a clear conscience about serving God? I believe having a Soul Goal and working towards reaching that goal by setting daily, weekly, and even monthly objectives for you to accomplish will ensure that just like Paul writes to Timothy, one day you will be able to say I know I have served God with a clear conscience as well.

Internal Conflict

When Christians fail to participate in the Great Commission and furthermore, prioritize other goals in their life as being of higher importance than the mission God has called them to, the result is most often an internal conflict overridden by living out the will of self, versus living out the will of our Heavenly Father. This most often causes a devastating loss of passion for the Gospel and sense of lack of purpose in life. Jesus' total and complete purpose in life while on the earth was to do the will of his heavenly Father (John 6:38). As followers of Jesus, we should seek to live out the will of our Heavenly Father, too. Establishing a Soul Goal and working towards it throughout your lifetime will help you to stay focused on doing the will of your Heavenly Father. In doing so, I believe it will help keep the passion for the Gospel and a sense of individual purpose in life alive and well inside of you.

Thief's Purpose vs. God's Purpose for Your Life

The thief's purpose is to steal and kill and destroy. My purpose is to give them a rich and satisfying life. (John 10:10 NLT)

God wants you to have a rich and satisfying life. And if, God willing, you are able to get to the end of your life and look back, he wants you to feel like you did have a rich and satisfying life. The question you must ask yourself then is this: with the path you are on right now, are you going to be able to say that? In other words, is there anything you could be doing right now to ensure yourself that in the end, your life will amount to a rich and satisfying one like God wants you to have? I think so.

If we know God wants us to have a rich and satisfying life, then we can conclude, perhaps, that if we live long enough, what Jesus tells us to do in this life will lead to a rich and satisfying one. It is important to note, the usage of the word rich here is referring more to rich as in being full, than it is to rich meaning earthly wealth. For example, think of something that could be described as rich, as in rich chocolate, meaning full of flavor.

So, the questions become: what does Jesus tell you to do throughout your life, specifically throughout your daily activities? And furthermore, are you doing them?

Here are a few of them...

God says:
1. Seek first the Kingdom of God (Matthew 6:33)
World says:
1. Seek first the kingdom of you

God says:
2. Set your mind on heaven (above) (Colossians 3:2)
World says:
2. Set your mind on things in earth (below)

God says:
3. Go make disciples...Win souls (Matthew 28:19)
World says:
3. Be a disciple of the world (be conformed to things of the world)

Just thinking about these three examples, it is pretty clear to see that they really are opposites of each other. Doing one or the other also produces opposite results. We know the thief's purpose is to steal, kill, and destroy. Doing the things of this world, results in submitting to the purpose of the enemy for your life which, in turn, will leave you with a very unsatisfying and empty life. However, doing what God has called you to do, will lead to a rich and satisfying life. Realize the pursuit of reaching a Soul Goal is seeking first the Kingdom of God, setting your mind on heaven, and telling others about, and making disciples of Jesus!

Did you know, one of the greatest things that Jesus told you to do as a Christian, which I believe is a vital key to living a rich and fulfilling life for any Christian, is the Great commission? That is, telling others about Jesus and making disciples of them. Interestingly enough, even though as Christians we are commanded to do it, and doing it is a vital key to living a rich and fulfilling life, I have heard it estimated that as low as only 2% of all Christians are actually actively engaged in carrying out the Great Commission on a regular basis. Wow! If that number is true, as a Christian, you must take a hard, honest look at yourself and try to understand if you are personally a part of the silent, inactive majority. It is my hope that this book helps you to do just that. In addition, if you come to the conclusion that you are silent and inactive in this area of your Christian life, it is my hope you will set a Soul Goal and begin to actively work towards achieving it. In doing this, you will not be inactive and silent anymore and, I believe, you will be well on your way to living the truly rich and satisfying life that God has for you, that can only be achieved by doing what God has called you to do.

Did You Even Have a Goal?

Imagine that you are standing before the Lord. He begins to show you all the goals you had throughout your lifetime and the accomplishments that resulted because of those goals; accomplishments pertaining to career, family, house, car, money, etc. When, all of a sudden, he asks you, "knowing that I gave you the mission to tell others about me in order that they may receive salvation, what was your goal for the number of people you wanted to reach?"

I don't know about you, but I don't want to have goals in my life to accomplish what my personal desires are for my career, family, finances, etc. and not have a goal for accomplishing what God has given me to do with my time here on earth in reaching souls. *For we must all appear before the judgment seat of Christ, so that each of us may receive what is due us for the things done while in the body, whether good or bad* (2 Corinthians 5:10). And on that day, perhaps you and I should at least have a goal we were working towards reaching in the mission God has given each and every one of us to complete. I don't know exactly what the experience will be like when we stand before the Lord and give this account to him, but I believe thinking about how I just described it sheds light on perhaps the importance of having a Soul Goal as a Christian in comparison to all the other goals we tend to set for ourselves. Do you at least have a Soul Goal? If not, learn how to set one now...

CHAPTER SEVEN

_____

Steps to <u>Setting</u> Your Soul Goal

Think about it... no matter what situation in life you are in, if you are reading this book, most likely you have the ability to have, set, and work towards the most important goal you could ever have in life... a Soul Goal. Think about all the other goals you have had throughout your lifetime. Think about all the goals you have for your life from this point moving forward. I encourage you to think about the value in having a Soul Goal compared to all the other goals you have accomplished, and all the other goals you are currently working towards. In addition to all your other goals, consider setting a Soul Goal and just like your other goals, take action in working towards achieving it. Next you will learn the steps I recommend taking in order to set a Soul Goal in your life!

Step 1. Understand and Accept that as a Christian, you have a responsibility to disciple and tell others about Jesus.

Step 2. Decide Once and For All you are going to make telling others a priority in your life and when opportunities arise to do so, you are going to seize the opportunity, even if it initially means stepping outside of your comfort zone. (Hint: the more you do it, the more comfortable you become in discipling and telling others about Jesus. Also, you will discover and develop a unique aspect in your personal relationship with God that can only be discovered and developed through you engaging in soul winning).

Step 3. Meditate on the Great Commission and the Prayer of Jabez.

Step 4. Pray. Spend time in prayer asking God to give you a specific number. First think in terms of life-long number.

Step 5. Once you get a specific number, Write it Down.

Step 6. Fill out the Soul Goal Certificate and hang it somewhere you will see it every day.

Step 1. <u>Understand and Accept</u>

Understand and accept, the moment you became a Christian you were given a mission to go and make disciples of others as well. Think about it, what is a mission without at least a goal and an objective? That is one of the reasons why I believe, simply, that defining clear individual goals and objectives for yourself in this mission will help you to carry out the mission God has given you.

Mission = Go tell and make disciples
Soul Goal = Reach "x" number of people
Objectives = Give to missions, ministry and evangelism; speak to others about Jesus, invite people to church, invite people over for dinner, invite people to church events, go on a Missions trip, pray for others, etc.

Commitment Level

And may your hearts be fully committed to the LORD our God, to live by his decrees and obey his commands, as at this time." (1 Kings 8:61)

You have probably heard the term "fully committed" before. Have you ever taken the time to really think about what that implies? It seems to suggest you could be committed to something, yet not fully committed to it. In other words, you are only partially committed.

Think about these scenarios for a few minutes: what if God was not fully committed to you? Or, what if you were only partially committed to your job, and your boss or employer knew it? Or, what if you were not fully committed to your marriage? Do you think any of these scenarios would be a good thing? Of course not.

But how do we know how committed someone is to something or someone? Most often, the answer is by looking at the person's actions. God has proven he is fully committed to us by sending his one and only son to earth to pay the ransom for our sins. If you are not very productive at work or you only show up half the time, perhaps this would indicate you are not fully committed to your job. If you abused your spouse or were unfaithful to him or her, maybe this would indicate you are not fully committed to your marriage. Our actions are often a great indicator of how committed we actually are to something, or someone.

With this in mind, think about your commitment level to the Great Commission as a Christian. When thinking about your commitment level to it, think about what actions you take in your daily life that are a direct result of this commitment. Now that you have thought about it for a few moments, how would you rate your commitment level? Using a rating scale from 1 to 10, 1 indicating a low commitment and 10 being fully committed, how would you rate yourself? Be honest with yourself. Is there any room for improvement?

I don't know about you, but I want to be fully committed to the mission at hand that God has given me. I hope you do too. I have found that consciously prioritizing those things that are important to me and taking specific actions towards them, helps me to stay fully committed to the things that really matter to me the most, like my relationship with the Lord, my marriage, my job, my family, reaching others with the Gospel, etc. A few of the actions that reflect my full commitment to these things could be praying, reading the Bible, going to church, spending time with my family, being faithful, being on time, doing my best at work, writing this book, and more.

With that said, I don't think any Christian wants to purposely be only partially committed to the Great Commission, especially knowing it is a mission that God himself has given each and every one of us a personal responsibility to carry out. Having the desire as a Christian to being fully committed to that which God has called you to (the Great Commission), what actions are you taking to show your full commitment to it? I believe setting a Soul Goal and then completing daily, weekly, and even monthly objectives in working toward this goal is a great way to ensure you are taking specific actions in your daily life that reflect your full commitment to reaching others with the message of the Gospel.

The first step to setting a Soul Goal in your life is fully accepting your responsibility as a Christian to the Great Commission to reach others with the message of the Gospel. Once you accept that it is your responsibility, you can further move forward towards setting a goal towards fulfilling your responsibility.

Step 2. <u>Decide Once and For All</u>

Decide you are going to make telling others the Gospel a priority in your life, and when opportunities arise to do so, you are going to seize the opportunity, even if it initially means stepping outside of your comfort zone. (Hint: the more you do it, the more comfortable you become in discipling and telling others about Jesus. Also, you will discover and develop a unique aspect in your personal relationship with God that can only be discovered and developed through you engaging in soul winning).

Many times as Christians we find ourselves in a situation where a clear opportunity to share the Gospel with someone arises. However, often times, when this happens we don't speak up when the opportunity presents itself. We stay silent. We don't act. We don't take advantage of the opportunity to speak into someone's life that could literally change their life forever. After the moment passes, we say to ourselves… "That was the perfect opportunity. I should have said something. I blew it." You could even have a sense of failure sweep over you in the immediate aftermath of these missed opportunities.

Even though we know as Christians we are commanded to share the Gospel with others, in the heat of the moment we simply don't engage and therefore, opportunity after opportunity goes by and the more we get comfortable with not engaging, the easier it becomes to not act in these situations.

But that is not how it is supposed to be. The Bible clearly speaks to our mission in life as Christian's to reach the world around us. Not only does the Bible speak about it, I believe when someone receives Christ into their life, they inherently have the desire placed inside of them to want to see other people come to have a living relationship with the Lord as well. There are many different reasons as to why we, maybe you, let these opportunities pass by without boldly speaking up. However, many of them have much to do with the mindset of the Christian.

One strategy that I highly encourage you to use is this: Decide Once And For All. Make the decision once, right now, that you are going to speak up in any future situations where an opportunity arises to share the Gospel. Now that you have decided, it is settled. The next time you find yourself with an opportunity to share the Gospel with someone, you don't have to go back and forth in your mind trying to decide whether or not you are going to in the heat of that moment. Why? Because remember, you just made the decision right now when you are not in the heat of the moment. Decide once and for all today, right now, and then spend the rest of your life managing that decision. Be a good manager by deciding once and for all you are going to take action with every opportunity that comes your way that will help you reach your Soul Goal!

Step 3. <u>Meditate on the Great Commission & Prayer of Jabez</u>

The Great Commission
Then the eleven disciples went to Galilee, to the mountain where Jesus had told them to go. When they saw him, they worshiped him; but some doubted. Then Jesus came to them and said, "All authority in heaven and on earth has been given to me. Therefore go and make disciples of all nations, baptizing them in the name of the Father and of the Son and of the Holy Spirit, and teaching them to obey everything I have commanded you. And surely I am with you always, to the very end of the age." (Matthew 28:16-20)

Prayer of Jabez
Jabez cried out to the God of Israel, "Oh, that you would bless me and enlarge my territory! Let your hand be with me, and keep me from harm so that I will be free from pain." And God granted his request. (1 Chronicles 4:10)

Now that you have decided once and for all you are going to seize every opportunity God brings across your path to reach and win others with the message of the Gospel, I recommend spending some time focusing your mind on the Great Commission. Think about the significance of it, what it means to you, what it means to others who have never accepted or even heard the Gospel before, what your life would be like if no one ever told you about it, etc.

After that, think about the prayer Jabez prayed. That God would bless him. That God would enlarge his territory. That God's hand would be with him. That God would keep him from harm so that he would be free from pain. Think about how God gave Jabez what he requested.

Step 4. <u>Pray About Your Number</u>

Spend time in prayer asking God to give you a specific number. First think in terms of life-long number.

As you pray in regards to setting a specific Soul Goal number, remember that there is a distinction between *reach* and *win*. Some people reading this book may want to set a goal for the number of souls (people) they want to *reach* with the message of the Gospel of Jesus Christ. Others may want to go a little further and set a goal for the number of souls (people) they *win* to the Kingdom of God. The difference is that setting a number for the amount of people you want to reach, does not necessarily specify how many people you are trying to understand accepted salvation through you reaching them. However, setting a Soul Goal for the number of people you want to win means you are setting a number for the amount of people you want to see accept salvation through Jesus Christ by your efforts. Whether you choose to pray about and set your Soul Goal based on the number of people you want to reach or win is up to you. Just know that when you are praying and seeking God about a number for your Soul Goal, you are clear about whether the number is for the amount of people you are going to reach or win.

I Challenge You to Ask

"So I say to you: Ask and it will be given to you; seek and you will find; knock and the door will be opened to you. For everyone who asks receives; the one who seeks finds; and to the one who knocks, the door will be opened.

(Luke 11:9-10)

Prayer is vital to having a relationship with God. Prayer is also extremely important to setting your Soul Goal. Why? Because this is not something you are doing on your own. Telling other people about Jesus and making them disciples is called a Co-Mission for a reason. I believe the fullness of what God has in store for you to be able to accomplish in reaching others with the message of salvation can only be accomplished with God helping you to do so. In other words, he has given you a mission in life that can only be fully accomplished with his help. Simply put, you cannot do it on your own without Him, nor should you want or even try, too. It's a Co-Mission, you co-laboring with Christ to accomplish his master plan for you and all humanity.

Therefore, it makes sense that you should pray and ask God what goal he would have you set towards reaching others. My suggestion is to think about and pray over your Soul Goal over several days, or longer if necessary. Pray until you really feel God has given you a specific number. Pray until you feel you have a peace and assurance that the number that keeps coming to your mind is the one. Once you have the number, don't second guess it. No matter how big or small it may be, accept it and begin to pursue it.

Numbers Matter to God – Be Specific

Numbers matter to God. Actually, numbers really matter to you too if you think about it. Don't believe me? Okay, what if you had $10,000 dollars in your bank account today, but when you checked it tomorrow it only showed you had $1,000 dollars? Somehow, there was a computer glitch and they deleted a zero from the total amount you had in your account. Would you simply not care? Of course not. Why? Because specific numbers matter to you.

Specific numbers matter to God also. After all, there is even a complete book in the Bible called Numbers. And what do you think you will find in that book? You guessed it, very specific numbers, and lots of them.

When praying about your Soul Goal, ask God to give you a specific number. Do not have the vague attitude of... 'God, I believe you for lots of souls' or 'God, use me to win a lot of souls for you.' These statements are far too vague. Furthermore, what may be a lot to you is different from what is a lot to me, which is still different than what is a lot to God.

When I first answered the question, what is my Soul Goal, I must admit I answered with one of these vague statements. It was complete and utter foolishness, especially with having all the experience I did in business and knowing the importance of setting specific goals.

A wise business owner or manager knows their numbers, and knows them well. They can tell you exactly how good or bad the business is doing based on the numbers produced by the company. Furthermore, a vitally important activity and strategy towards creating success in business, as well as in life, is setting specific goals and working towards reaching them. Maybe you have even worked in a job where your boss has given you a specific number goal to reach in whatever you are doing. Providing you with this specific number gives you an exact target to work towards. Without it, you may not be motivated or stretched to reach your full potential. In addition, without a specific goal it is very difficult to see how well you are doing, or not, in working towards a specific objective. In other words, without a specific goal, you or your company may fail to reach the objectives necessary to stay on a path leading to success.

Why do I say it was foolishness when I answered "God use me to win lots of souls in my lifetime"? Think about it. This is such a vague, non-specific answer. In my business, I would never set a goal that way. Why? Because how would I measure the success of what I was trying to accomplish if I never set a specific number attached to it? In addition, how would I push and motivate myself toward steady growth and success if I didn't specifically know what I was growing towards and what number I had identified that I needed to reach in order to be successful?

Simply put, one of the most valuable attributes to setting a specific number to a goal is that it enables you to identify whether your actions are effective or not in doing what you are trying to do. The hard truth is, I wonder if many Christians (like how I once was) don't want to put a specific number to a Soul Goal, because doing so would give them a clearer picture on whether or not they are doing what God has called them to do in reaching others with the message of the Gospel. Putting a specific number to the responsibility and task God has given them would cause them to have to come to terms with the reality of their inactivity in the mission God has given them in life. The reality that, they may be failing at the mission. And sadly for some, they would rather not come to terms with the reality of their inactivity to reach others with the message of the Gospel.

My hope and prayer today, is that, this is not you. I hope it is your heart, intent, and will to do everything God has called you to do to the best of your ability. Holding nothing back and charging forward with all sincerity, desire, commitment, and motivation to do the will of the Father on earth as it is in Heaven. And whether or not you think having a Soul Goal will personally help you know how well you are doing just that, continue to look for ways that you may measure and know with certainty that you are living out your maximum God-given potential. Specific numbers matter to God and in most cases, specific numbers matter if you are going to try to measure the successes or failures of your actions. If you are going to set a Soul Goal, do not vaguely say "I want to win a lot of souls for God in my lifetime." Rather, set a specific, finite number and start working towards reaching it. In doing this, I believe you will be well on your way to accomplishing the specific mission God has given you in the mission of reaching others with the greatest message the world has ever know, the message of love, grace, forgiveness of sins, salvation, and reconciliation for all unto God.

Does the Size of Your Goal Matter?

Does the size of your Soul Goal matter? Let me first say this, I have no idea what the number of your Soul Goal should be. Whatever number you put to your Soul Goal is first and foremost between you and God. Why? Because God created you, placed you on this earth, and gave you the mission to reach souls. Simply put, he gave you the mission. Not me, your pastor, your friend, or anyone else. Even though we are co-laborers in the body of Christ together, we each have our own individual responsibility to the Great Commission of reaching others with the message of the Gospel.

The question you may have is this, what if my number is significantly smaller than someone else's, or what if my number is significantly larger than someone else's? Is either of them good or bad, right or wrong? Understand, putting a specific number to your Soul Goal is very important. If you are going to set a Soul Goal, you must put a finite, specific number to it. However, you should not determine what your number should be based off of what someone else's Soul Goal is. Instead, pray and seek the Lord for what he would have you do. Once you feel quite confident and have a sense of 'knowing' what your number should be, that's it. Whether or not your number is big or small compared to other peoples' numbers does not matter when you have a confidence in knowing what God has given you.

The size of your Soul Goal number only matters between you and God. If you have an honest and clear conscience that the goal you have set is correct, do not allow yourself to become discouraged when you hear the Soul Goal of others. Likewise, do not be boastful towards others about your Soul Goal in a way that would cause them to be discouraged about theirs. Instead, rejoice with one another having an attitude of humility and gratefulness, building each other up in the things of the Lord so each is better able to fulfill the goal they have put the hearts, hands, and mind too.

And remember, this is extremely important; do not try to run off and complete reaching your goal without God.

Don't Try Without God

The LORD is my strength and my shield; my heart trusts in him, and he helps me. My heart leaps for joy, and with my song I praise him. (Psalm 28:7)

Extremely Important… Once you set a number to your Soul Goal, do not try to run off and complete it without God. As Christians, it is funny how we often try to do this when God gives us something to do. In our zeal to want to please the Lord, we run off towards accomplishing the task at hand and leave God behind. Simply put, we try to accomplish it in our own might. When doing this, it often leads to frustration, disappointment, and sometimes even failure. It's not so much that we heard God wrong, as it is that we simply left Him behind in trying to accomplish something he gave us to do that could only be accomplished working together with Him and not on our own.

Do not make this same mistake when it comes to your Soul Goal. Approach working towards your Soul Goal by taking actions in faith believing that God is going to help you reach your daily objectives. View your Soul Goal as actually being a tool that helps your relationship with the Lord grow stronger and stronger, closer and closer together as you daily make it a priority to work together to reach others with his never-failing, all consuming, unconditional love. It is called a Co-Mission for a reason, and just because you set a personal number towards your Soul Goal doesn't mean the mission changes to a solo-mission.

Setting Your Soul Goal Too Small

What happens if you set your Soul Goal too small? First of all, remember that your Soul Goal should be the goal you are working towards throughout your entire lifetime. However, it is my experience that when you get serious about reaching souls for the

Kingdom of God, he can get quite serious about enabling you to reach a goal quicker than what you had ever thought possible, especially when it comes to soul winning. It would not be uncommon for you to set your Soul Goal after having prayed about it and getting a confidence in it, that soon after you start working towards it you realize you may reach your goal a lot quicker than what you initially thought.

That's okay. As you begin to work towards your Soul Goal, most likely you will start to see God working in your life and through you to reach others on a level you had never experienced before. When this happens, your faith begins to grow and you begin to have the confidence and faith to believe God for even greater things. You begin to see the things that were once impossible for you, now possible with God's help.

In the case you set your Soul Goal too small, remember this phrase: if you reach it, you can always increase it! I believe your Soul Goal should have two attributes to it; it should be a goal that would stretch you beyond where you currently are, and it should be a goal that you would consider not necessarily easy to reach. Even with those two things in mind, know that when you commit to allowing God to use you in a specific way, like winning souls, he will often stretch you further than what you thought you could be stretched, and enable you to more easily reach what you thought was so difficult. However, whether too small or not, you may never understand what you just read if you never at least commit to a Soul Goal. Remember once again, if you reach it, you can always increase it. So, set a Soul Goal and begin working towards it as soon as possible and see for yourself... just what God can do!

What if I Ask and Don't Get a Response?

To the best of my knowledge there is nowhere in the Bible that says you must set a specific Soul Goal. However, we can recognize that setting goals in our lives helps us to achieve things that we really want, or need, to accomplish. Simply put, setting a specific goal towards something, whether it is for finances, career, retirement, house, car, or souls helps you achieve it in a more effective and efficient way than not having a goal at all. As we identify this principle, we will learn to understand the concept of utilizing goals to help stretch us and keep us focused on taking specific actions toward reaching a specific outcome. Although the Bible may not explicitly tell you to set a Soul Goal, I believe doing so can help you more efficiently and effectively do what God has clearly told us to do, which is reaching others with the message of salvation through Jesus Christ.

With that said, if you have earnestly sought the Lord through prayer and petition about setting a Soul Goal and what your number should be and you seemingly get no answer, or are still completely lost on what number you should set, you have two options: don't set a number at all, or set a number by faith. If you choose to not set a number at all, realize you still have an obligation to reach others for the Kingdom of God. Even though you may not have a specific number you are working towards, as a Christian, continue to look for opportunities throughout your daily life to be actively engaged in the Great Commission to reach others for the Kingdom of God. However, if you choose to set a Soul Goal by faith even though you are not quite confident of the specific number God wants you to have, I believe God will honor your sincere desire to want to reach others in one of the most efficient and effective ways you know how. Aligning the desire of your heart with the desire of God's heart to see souls saved by choosing to set a Soul Goal even though you are not quite sure what the number should be, I believe, shows a deep level of commitment and faith towards your desire to want to serve the Lord with your whole life. In this, I believe the Lord is well-pleased.

Step 5. <u>Write it Down – Extremely Important</u>

Do not just keep your Soul Goal in your mind. There is something powerful that happens when you actually hand-write a goal down yourself, which is exactly what you should do with your Soul Goal. Studies have shown that when people put their goals in handwriting, they are drastically much more likely to work towards reaching them and furthermore, much more likely to be successful at accomplishing them. So, knowing that, hand-write your Soul Goal down yourself and place it somewhere you will see it every day from now on. You could even put it in multiple locations like in your bedroom, living room, car, office, or phone. One creative idea I highly suggest doing is writing this number on our Soul Goal Certificate, framing it, and hanging it on the wall in your home.

Step 6. <u>Fill Out the Soul Goal Certificate</u>

Write the vision, and make it plain upon tables, that he may run that readeth it. (Habakkuk 2:2 KJV)

Take it a step further...

Because your Soul Goal is now one of the most important goals you are going to be working towards accomplishing in your life, I recommend filling out our Soul Goal certificate, framing it, and hanging it on the wall of your house or wherever you live. You could even hang it in a place where not only you are going to see it every day, but when you have visitors over they will see it too. It may spark up an interesting conversation. One that will either encourage other fellow Christians to have a Soul Goal as well, or one that will open the door for you to witness to someone who is not a follower of Christ yet. You never know, doing this may just help you get one more person closer to reaching your Soul Goal.

Get a Soul Goal Certificate here... www.SoulGoalBook.com

<u>TRACK YOUR PROGRESS</u>

Place a check mark next to each step as you complete them...

- O Understand and Accept Your Responsibility as a Christian to The Great Commission
- O Decide Once and For All to Seize Opportunities to Reach and Win Others
- O Meditate on the Great Commission and the Prayer of Jabez
- O Pray for Your Specific Soul Goal Number
- O Write Down Your Number
- O Fill Out the Soul Goal Certificate at www.SoulGoalBook.com

CHAPTER EIGHT

_____

Steps to <u>Reaching</u> Your Soul Goal

Do you not know that in a race all the runners run, but only one gets the prize? Run in such a way as to get the prize. Everyone who competes in the games goes into strict training. They do it to get a crown that will not last, but we do it to get a crown that will last forever. Therefore I do not run like someone running aimlessly (1 Corinthians 9:24-26)

Whether you feel like God has given you a specific number or you have come up with a number by faith on your own, hopefully by now have a Soul Goal. After writing it down and placing it somewhere you will see often, now it is time to start actively working towards reaching your specific Soul Goal! The following are a few action steps I have identified to help you do just that. Taking the following steps will help you systematically and strategically become organized in your actions as you begin to pursue your Soul Goal.

When it comes to being organized, I understand that there are two types of people in this world; ones who are well organized and others who are not. No matter which category you find yourself in, I encourage you to at least read through the following action steps and, at minimum, understand their basic concepts. Whether you want to approach reaching your Soul Goal by organizing your actions down to the day, or you want to take a whole different approach altogether, the choice is yours. The important thing is, now that you have a Soul Goal don't just do nothing. Read the following steps and begin taking action towards reaching your goal of eternal impact in the lives of others for the Kingdom of God.

Step 1. Determine Your Starting Point

Step 2. Break down your life-long Soul Goal into shorter weekly, monthly, and yearly goals

Step 3. Determine Objectives

Step 1. <u>Determine Your Starting Point</u>

Now that you have a Soul Goal, the first step in strategically taking action towards reaching it is determining your starting point. In other words, where do you stand today in terms of reaching others? This is important for you to know because as you proceed through the following action steps, you will be setting shorter goals and objectives for your first year working toward your life-long Soul Goal based off of your starting point.

Evaluating Where You Are Now

Spend some time thinking about your Soul Goal and ask yourself how many souls are you currently reaching or winning per week, month, or year?

One way to getting an idea of where you currently stand in terms of soul winning is to think back over the last week, month, and year. Are there any particular moments or people that stand out in your mind? Do you regularly give to missions, evangelism or ministry work specifically meant to reach and win people? Do you volunteer a certain amount of your time to ministry-type work? Anything else you can think of? Whatever you can identify that you currently do that reaches or wins souls, write it down. If it is people you have spoken too, money you have given, or the amount of time you have volunteered, try to understand how much time, money, and/or effort you currently put into reaching others for the Kingdom of God. Spend a few minutes thinking about that now and write it all down. See the worksheet in this book!

As you are thinking about it, now is also a good time to praise and thank God for using you to touch the lives of others! If you cannot think of a single action, moment or person that God has used you to reach or win someone in the recent past, begin to pray and ask God to use you from this point going forward. Begin to thank Him for all the people he is going to send across your path in the near future that you will have an opportunity to share the Gospel with.

Now that you have set your mind on thinking about that, there may even be some other people or moments that come to mind in the next several days that you haven't thought about right now. If that happens, make sure to write those down too. There is something about writing these actions, moments and people down that causes you to value, think about, and praise God more than you would if you didn't write them down at all. Don't skip the process of writing these down. It will surely build your faith and excitement to win even more people going forward.

Many of you have probably never thought about or done this before. However, when you do, you will most likely surprise yourself in one of two ways. The first will leave you pleasantly surprised by the amount of time, money, and actions that God has used you to reach people that you totally forgot about, or you will be unpleasantly surprised and realize that you really haven't allowed God to use you much at all to touch the lives of others in the recent weeks, months, or years.

No matter what the result of this personal reflection for you is, good or bad, it is extremely important for you to come to terms with knowing exactly where you stand today in order that you may improve upon your efforts tomorrow. You must have a starting point. And going through this process of looking back and evaluating yourself should help you clearly define your starting point by which you are going to move forward towards reaching your Soul Goal from here.

In summary, when looking back over the past weeks, months, or year, try to come up with actual numbers in regards to your soul reaching or winning efforts as a Christian. Don't worry, sometimes it is difficult to know for sure, and in reality, the numbers could be a little less or a little more than what you actually did, but it is important to come up with actual, finite numbers. Whether it is zero, one hundred, or more, be honest with yourself and come up with numbers on where you currently stand in order to stretch yourself to set goals and objectives to do even more moving forward.

Business Model for Success

Think about this: successful businesses always look to improve at least a little bit beyond what they did the previous quarter or even year. In order to evaluate whether or not they are improving and moving forward, businesses must have a starting point to then measure their efforts from that point moving forward. A company that perhaps started out very small ten years ago, and over time constantly and consistently gradually stretched their goals a little more and a little more each time, eventually results in a company today that is far greater and achieving far more than when they first started out. The goals they had ten years ago may today seem very small, nevertheless it took finding a starting point, setting a goal based off that starting point, and then gradually increasing the goal a little more each time they reached it.

As Christians, I believe we can use this same method and concept to evaluate our efforts and progress in reaching souls. Just like any successful business, we want to constantly keep growing and improving on our efforts over time to reach people with the message of the Gospel. The key is finding your starting point and moving forward from there.

After collecting any and all numbers you can think of in regards to your recent past efforts to reach or win souls, <u>calculate your final Starting Point number in terms of what you do per month. This per month calculation will be very important in Step 2.</u>

Once you have your Starting Point, you can proceed to Step 2 where you will begin to set short-term goals to accomplish within the next year toward your life-long Soul Goal.

Calculate Your Starting Point

Names of people you have witnessed to in the last week?

_____

Names of people you have witnessed to in the **last month?**

_____

Names of people you have witnessed to in the last 12 months?

_____

_____

Money you gave to missions last week?   _____

Money you gave to missions **last month?**   _____

Money you gave to missions last 12 months?   _____

How many people did you invite to church last week?   _____

How many people did you invite to church **last month?** _____

How many people did you invite to church last 12 months? _____

Amount of time you volunteered or worked at your church or other ministry **last month?**   _____

Amount of time you volunteered or worked at your church or other ministry last 12 months? _____

Other (any other special events, programs, or ministries you gave money to, worked at, volunteered your time with, or invited others to go to) in last 12 months?

_____

_____

How many souls did you reach/win (circle one) last week?   _____

How many souls did you reach/win (circle one) **last month?** _____

How many souls did you reach/win (circle one) last 12 months? _____

* Look at your impact over the last several months for each category above. Averaging them will give you the Starting Point by which you will set short-term goals to improve your efforts as you work towards your Soul Goal in your first year!

What is your Soul Goal? _____
(life-long number of people you want to win or reach)

Additional resources & more specific suggestions can be found at
www.SoulGoalBook.com

Step 2. <u>Create Short-Term Goals</u>

Urgency for Your Goal

You have decided the length of our lives. You know how many months we will live, and we are not given a minute longer. (Job 14:5 NLT)

One attribute associated with setting a goal that actually helps keep us motivated to reach the goal, is a sense of urgency. When you set a goal with a specific time restraint attached to it, you can often experience an increasing sense of urgency as the time draws closer and closer to running out. This sense of urgency can be strategically utilized by you in a positive way to help you reach your life-long Soul Goal. Realize most people have no idea of how long they have left to live on earth, including you. Only God specifically knows that. However, the Bible does say our days are numbered, meaning that you only have a specific number of days to reach your Soul Goal. Therefore, you should approach your Soul Goal with urgency; not continuously putting it off day after day, week after week, month after month, year after year. One way to keep a sense of urgency alive in your pursuit to reach your Soul Goal, is by creating short-term goals. Even though you may not know whether you have days, weeks, or years left to your life on earth, setting short-term goals is a way to keep a sense of urgency alive in your daily activities on a regular basis as you pursue your life-long Soul Goal.

Okay, at this point you have a Soul Goal number and you have a pretty good idea what your Starting Point is. The question is, how do you get from your Starting Point today to reaching your life-long Soul Goal by the end of your life? One way is by creating short-term goals you can easily reach, by identifying and taking actions toward completing strategic objectives. In step 2, I am going to explain how you can begin setting short-term goals in your life to keep you moving towards reaching your life-long Soul Goal. In other words, teaching you how to set short-term goals in your life to keeping you actively engaged in your responsibility and commitment to the Great Commission as a Christian, reaching others with the message of salvation through Jesus Christ.

As previously stated, I realize perhaps not everyone likes too, or even works effectively, by being organized in a very detailed manner towards accomplishing goals. Understand, there are many different ways in which you could go about working towards reaching your life-long Soul Goal. Knowing how you personally function well in reaching goals and implementing that into pursuing your Soul Goal is going to be a key to your success. Just know, if you want to become extremely well organized and detailed down to every single day in your approach to reaching or winning souls, that is certainly possible.

As I present the following ideas and concepts to you, decide what is going to work best for you and then create your own short-term goal plan. Make a plan that matches you well. One that will keep you on track toward success, yet not bog you down or set you up for failure.

Before I go any further, let me first clarify what I am talking about when I say short-term goal versus Soul Goal. Think of your Soul Goal as your life-long goal for reaching or winning souls. For the purposes of this book, a Soul Goal is a life-long, long-term goal (specific number). Short-term goals are number goals for souls as well, but are generally made for reaching or winning souls over a shorter period of time; such as weekly, monthly, quarterly, or yearly. Because a Soul Goal is in most cases, a goal that spans a vast number of years, I find it necessary to approach working towards a Soul Goal by breaking it down into smaller, easier to manage short-term goals. Among many other reasons, doing this helps keep you engaged in, focused on, and active towards reaching shorter time goals that incrementally will accumulate towards accomplishing your life-long Soul Goal.

Whether it is weekly, monthly, quarterly, or yearly, it is up to you to decide what time range you want to establish your short-term goals around. At a very minimum, I recommend setting a yearly goal for the number of souls you want to reach or win. However, know that in addition to setting a goal for the year, you could further break that goal down into quarterly, monthly, weekly, or even daily short-term goals. Simply put, short-term goals help keep you on track and focused in your day-to-day, week-to-week, month-to-month, and year-to-year activities to ensure your long-term success!

Here are some examples on how to start setting some short-term goals towards reaching your Soul Goal. In these examples, I use an example goal number for winning souls directly, but realize you should also set a goal for increasing anything you do that contributes to reaching or winning souls like giving money too, or volunteering your time towards missions, evangelism, and/or ministry.

1 Year Short-Term Goal

Now that you have identified your Starting Point (if you haven't yet, see Step 1), let's talk about setting your yearly goal. To keep things simple, make the starting point of your yearly goal January 1st every year and the ending point of your yearly goal December 31st every year. However, if this is your first time setting a yearly goal, start wherever you are in the year right now and end this year's goal on December 31st. For example, if you are reading this near the end of July, set your first-year goal based off of having five more months left in this year. Then next year, start your yearly goal from January 1st through December 31st. Repeat this every year for the rest of your life or until you reach your life-long Soul Goal.

How to determine what your *first* 1 year goal should be…

If this is your first year setting a 1 year short-term goal towards your Soul Goal, start by using your Starting Point. Now that you have a pretty good idea of where you are starting out based on finding your Starting Point through Step 1, determine what a good 1 year goal for you would be based on the remaining months left in this year. For example, if after calculating your Starting Point you determine that you are winning approximately 1 soul per month and there are 5 months left in the year, maybe you want to set your first year goal to try to win 2 souls per month for the next 5 months. Therefore, using your Starting Point, you have now set a goal that will stretch and challenge you to do more than what you are currently doing.

Once you get to December, you can begin thinking about setting a full 1 year short-term goal for next year!

How to determine what your 1 year goal should be…

Every year in December, evaluate how well you did towards reaching the 1 year goal you set for yourself to reach that year. Based on how well you did or not, set another 1 year goal for the upcoming year. Start working towards it as soon as possible come January 1st. For example, imagine you are now in December. If your 1 year short-term goal was to win 20 souls this year, determine whether or not you reached your goal. If you did not reach it, based on how close you came to reaching your goal, set another 1 year goal for the next year by either keeping the same goal to try to reach another 20 souls or slightly increase your goal from 20 to maybe 30. If you did reach your 1 year goal, determine how fast you reached it and by how much you went over it. If you reached your 1 year goal only six months into the year, maybe you should double or triple your 1 year goal for next year. In this example, if you had set your 1 year goal to win 20 souls and by six months into the year you had already won 20 souls, consider increasing your 1 year goal next year to 50 to 100 souls or more!

Weekly, Monthly, and Quarterly Short-Term Goals

You may want to consider setting a weekly, monthly, or quarterly goal for the number of people you want to try to reach in order to keep you on track with reaching your yearly goal

For those of you who want to further break down your 1 year goal into a weekly, monthly, and/or quarterly goal, that is certainly possible. Using the number you have set for your 1 year goal, determine how many souls that would be weekly, monthly or quarterly for you to reach. For example, if you set a 1 year goal to win 24 souls, that means your monthly goal would be to win 2 souls per month and your quarterly goal would be to win 6 souls per quarter. If it helps you to create these short-term goals based off your 1 year short-term goal, by all means do it. Remember, it is up to you to decide what is going to work best for you.

Once you have decided on what short-term goals you are going to set for yourself, proceed to Step 3 where I am going to introduce you to creating Objectives towards reaching your short-term goals.

Calculate Your *First* 1 Year Goal

How many months are left in this year (now – Dec.31) _____

How many souls will you reach/win (circle one) next __ months? _____
How many souls will you reach/win (circle one) **next month?** _____
How many souls will you reach/win (circle one) next week? _____

Names of people you will witness to in the **next month?**
_____
Names of people you will witness to over the remaining __ months?
_____
_____
Money you will give to missions next week? _____
Money you will give to missions **next month?** _____
Money you will give to missions remaining __ months? _____

How many people will you invite to church next week? _____
How many people will you invite to church **next month?** _____
How many people will you invite to church
remaining __ months? _____

Amount of time you will volunteer or work at your church or other
ministry **next month?** _____
Amount of time you will volunteer or work at your church or other
ministry remaining __ months? _____

Other (any other special events, programs, or ministries you will give
money to, work at, volunteer your time with, or invite others to go
to) **remaining __ months?**
_____
_____

* Looking at your Starting Point (from the Calculate Your Starting
Point worksheet) and set goals for the remainder of the year that are
going to help you increase your impact in reaching or winning others!

What is your Soul Goal? _____
(life-long number of people you want to win or reach)

Additional resources & more specific suggestions can be found at
www.SoulGoalBook.com

Calculate Your *Annual* 1 Year Goal

Your Annual Goal is a 12 month goal (Jan 1 – Dec.31)

What is your Soul Goal? _____
(life-long number of people you want to win or reach)

How many souls will you reach/win (circle one) next 12 months? _____
How many souls will you reach/win (circle one) next month?   _____
How many souls will you reach/win (circle one) next week?   _____

Names of people you will witness to in the next month?
_____

Names of people you will witness to over the next 12 months?
_____
_____

Money you will give to missions next week?   _____
Money you will give to missions next month?   _____
Money you will give to missions next 12 months?   _____

How many people will you invite to church next week?   _____
How many people will you invite to church next month?   _____
How many people will you invite to church next 12 months? _____

Amount of time you will volunteer or work at your church or other ministry next month? _____
Amount of time you will volunteer or work at your church or other ministry next 12 months? _____

Other (any other special events, programs, or ministries you will give money to, work at, volunteer your time with, or invite others to go to) next 12 months?
_____
_____

* This worksheet is intended to be used every year following the completion of your first year. Use it in December every year to set your short-term goals for the upcoming year as you plan to make an impact in reaching or winning others!

Additional resources & more specific suggestions can be found at
www.SoulGoalBook.com

Step 3. <u>Determine Objectives</u>

As previously discussed earlier in this book…

Objectives are exact steps you identify you want, or must take, to help you reach your goal. Simply put, objectives are action steps. They are designed to produce specific results within a specific amount of time. They clearly state what is to be achieved, how it is to be achieved, who is going to achieve it, and when it is to be achieved by. Think short-term deadlines and steps that must be taken to reach the deadlines. Objectives are easily measureable and are therefore, great indicators to how well you are doing towards reaching your overall goal.

Now that you have a life-long Soul Goal and shorter-term goals in place to give you a not-so-distant target to aim for, it is necessary to identify some action steps you can easily take to help you reach your goals. Think of the Objectives as the steps in your action plan to reach your goals within a certain amount of time.

For example, let's say your Soul Goal is to win 10,000 souls for the Kingdom of God from now until the end of your earthly life. You could then set yearly, quarterly, monthly, weekly, and even daily short term goals to keep you moving towards your life-long Soul Goal. (See worksheets)

See the following examples:
1 Year Goal – this year my goal is to win 60 souls.
Monthly Goal – because I have a yearly goal to win 60 souls, I am going to work towards winning 5 souls per month. (5 souls x 12 months = 60 souls in 1 year)
Weekly Goal – because I have a monthly goal to win 5 souls per month, I am going to work towards winning at least 1 soul per week. Some weeks I will try to win at least 2 per week.

Here is an example of the **Objectives** you could set towards reaching the previous Soul Goal example:

Objective 1. Invite at least 2 people to church with me every week.
Objective 2. Give xxx.xx amount of money to missions, ministry, or evangelism work every month.
Objective 3. Volunteer at least 1 weekend a month at your church.
Objective 4. Call at least 1 friend or family member per week on the phone and pray for them.
Objective 5. Invite at least 1 family over for dinner per month.
Objective 6. Bring at least 1 new person to my church small group or fellowship group per month.
Objective 7. Cook at least 1 meal every 2 weeks for someone in a difficult situation and bring it to them.
Objective 8. Invite at least 10 friends to every special church event or holiday this year.
Objective 9. Go on 1 Mission Trip with my church this year.
And so many more…

I think you can clearly see the idea by now. Objectives are all about identifying specific actions you can do and then being intentional in doing them. Notice, you could do all of the actions above, come up with your own ideas not listed here, or pick and choose between several of them. The key is, try to identify specific actions you are going to intentionally take towards completing your weekly, monthly, quarterly, or yearly goals.

Once again, whether your short-term goals are monthly, weekly, or daily goals, the key to success is clearly identifying what the number of souls is associated with the goal and furthermore, what the specific actions that you will take are to enable you to reach that number.

Setting Objectives
for this Year, Quarter, Month, or Week

Now that you know what Objectives are, begin to brainstorm ideas for objectives you would like to implement into reaching your short-term goals. You can use the objectives I listed previously or you can come up with your own. Think to yourself: "what specific actions am I going to take and how often am I going to take them in order to reach my short-term goals?" Create an Action Plan based off your short-term goals and the objectives you have decided you will complete to reach your goals. (See Action Plan worksheet)

Action Plan - Objectives

What is your Soul Goal? _____
(life-long number of people you want to win or reach)

How many souls will I reach/win (circle one) next 12 months? _____
How many souls will I reach/win (circle one) next month? _____
How many souls will I reach/win (circle one) next week? _____

How many people will I invite to church next 12 months? _____
How many people will I invite to church next month? _____
How many people will I invite to church next week? _____

Money I will give to missions next 12 months? _____
Money I will give to missions next month? _____
Money I will give to missions next week? _____

Names of people I will witness to in the next month?

_____

Names of people I will witness to over the next 12 months?

_____

_____

Amount of time I will volunteer or work at my church or other ministry next week? _____
Amount of time I will volunteer or work at my church or other ministry next month? _____
Amount of time you I volunteer or work at my church or other ministry next 12 months? _____

Number of people I will call next week? _____
Number of people I will call next month? _____
Number of people I will call next 12 months? _____

Number of people I will invite to a meal next week? _____
Number of people I will invite to a meal next month? _____
Number of people I will invite to a meal next 12 months? _____

Number of people I will bring to Bible study next week? _____
Number of people I will bring to Bible study next month? _____
Number of people I will bring to Bible study next 12 months? _____

I will go on a Mission Trip this year? Y/N

Number of people I will bring to church special events next 12 months? _____

Other (any other special events, programs, or ministries I will give money to, work at, volunteer my time with, or invite others to go to) next 12 months?

_____

_____

* This worksheet is intended to help you identify specific actions you can take to help you reach your short-term goals and ultimately your Soul Goal. It is by no means a list of all the actions you could take…just a few ideas to help you get started!

Additional resources & more specific suggestions can be found at
www.SoulGoalBook.com

Calendar

Another strategy you may want to consider when creating your Objectives is to get out a calendar and start looking at the upcoming year. Make special note of certain holidays like Easter and Christmas, and others that you may want to plan for in advance. In addition, there are special days in almost every month you can strategically plan objectives and actions around to help you reach your short-term goals. Planning your soul winning objectives around holidays and special days of the year is a great way to have a maximum impact in reaching people while keeping in step with the seasons of the year.

If you think about it, you will realize that many retail stores and businesses use this exact strategy. Whether you visit their website or physically step foot inside their store, you will notice that their marketing, decorations, and featured products all have a common theme that reflects the season or upcoming holiday. They strategically plan in advance to make this happen. Why? Because it works. And even though as Christians we are not ultimately trying to simply sell someone a product, I believe we can use this same strategy in keeping in step with special days, seasons, or holidays to plan our soul winning efforts around, to enable us to have a strategic impact in the lives of others.

Here are some examples: invite friends and neighbors to your house for an Easter Egg hunt. At the event, tell the real meaning behind Easter and invite people to your church or offer to pray for anyone that wants it. At Christmas, buy gifts for someone you know who is really in need or having a hard time in life. As you are giving the gifts, offer to pray with them.

There are so many creative ideas you could come up with to strategically plan to reach others with the message of the Gospel by planning your actions, activities, invites, or events around holidays or others special days in the year. The key is to plan ahead and incorporate this strategy into your objectives to reach your short-term goals of reaching others with the love and message of Jesus Christ.

Your Church Events

In addition, look at your church events and try to incorporate them into your strategy to reach your Soul Goal by including them in the objectives toward reaching your short-term goals. For example, maybe you go to a Bible study every week. You could mark these on your calendar for the whole year and set a goal to invite at least 1 person a week to come to the Bible study with you. If your church puts on any type of production or play throughout the year, or does any community outreaches, you can plan ahead now and incorporate them into your Action Plan as well.

There are many different ideas, activities, and actions you could incorporate into an Action Plan you design to reach your short-term goals. How specific and detailed you want to get with your plans and objectives is up to you. However, if you decide to create a well-thought-out plan like this, try breaking it down by daily, weekly, and monthly objectives and actions you are going to take to reach those objectives.

For some people, creating a step-by-step plan with specific goals and objectives is necessary to keep them motivated and on track with the Soul Goal they have set. However, for other people, a step-by-step plan like this will be more of a distraction than a benefit to them. It is up to you to decide whether you need to create a plan like this for yourself or not. The key is, honestly do whatever you feel you need to do to ensure you make steady progress toward and keep actively engaged in your Soul Goal to reach others with the message of the Gospel.

REMINDERS

Once you have a list of Objectives and have placed them within the context of your short-term goals, below are a few ideas you can use to help remind yourself of your daily, weekly, and monthly objectives.

Daily To-Do List

What is on your daily to-do list? Having a daily, weekly, or even monthly to-do list is an important strategy and discipline many people use to ensure that they "get stuff done." There are many people who are actually quite lost if they don't have this list to keep them on track. These simple lists, often times, are in-part, a determining factor between someone who is able to use their time efficiently, effectively, and wisely versus someone who is not. One strategy to having a successful to-do list is to prioritize the list in terms of items that are most important down to items that are least important. In addition, items can be arranged by time sensitivity. Meaning, you can arrange items on the list by how soon they need to be completed.

Here is a quick thought: although having a to-do list can be quite a useful tool to keep us on track while living such busy lives, as a Christian, when is the last time you put at the top of your to-do list the number of people you wanted God to use you that day, or that week to be able to reach?

You see, even with something so simple as a to-do list, it becomes so easy for us as Christians to get caught up in prioritizing our life in terms of things that seem important to us at the moment, yet we forget about the most important mission God has called each and every one of us to in life, which is reaching other people with the Good News of the Gospel. I am not saying that you don't have very important, high priority items that should be at the top of your list, because I am sure you do. But the next time you go to make out that to-do list, consider writing at the top of your list, above anything else, an objective to complete for the number of souls you want God to use you to reach that day, week, or even month! When you prioritize reaching souls as the most important thing in your life, you will be amazed at how God begins to work in your life to not only enable you to reach your Soul Goal, but to help you reach so many of your other goals as well.

Cell Phone Reminders

Look at your list of Objectives. Place some, or all of your Objectives, as cell phone reminders. That way, if you get busy or caught up by other things in life, your phone can remind you of certain objectives you have set to stay active in and on track towards reaching people for the Kingdom of God. I'd say as a Christian, what an amazing cell phone reminder to have!

Physical Calendar or Day Planner

I know what you're thinking, "do people actually still carry these around?" And the answer is yes, I would be one of those people. Even though I do like technology and set cell phone reminders myself, I still like to have a paper hard-copy calendar and planner with me. If this is representative of you too, I encourage you to write down your short-term goals and objectives in them.

Anchored In Prayer

It is important to understand that even though you may set a Soul Goal and take physical actions by faith to reach that goal, like setting short-term goals and objectives, much of our battle is fought through prayer. The goal for souls is a spiritual battle. Therefore, the power of prayer cannot be overstated in its necessity to be used by you in reaching others with the Good News of Jesus Christ. Simply put, your Soul Goal must be anchored in prayer.

Finally, be strong in the Lord and in his mighty power. Put on the full armor of God, so that you can take your stand against the devil's schemes. For our struggle is not against flesh and blood, but against the rulers, against the authorities, against the powers of this dark world and against the spiritual forces of evil in the heavenly realms. Therefore put on the full armor of God, so that when the day of evil comes, you may be able to stand your ground, and after you have done everything, to stand. Stand firm then, with the belt of truth buckled around your waist, with the breastplate of righteousness in place, and with your feet fitted with the readiness that comes from the gospel of peace. In addition to all this, take up the shield of faith, with which you can extinguish all the flaming arrows of the evil one. Take the helmet of salvation and the sword of the Spirit, which is the word of God. And pray in the Spirit on all occasions with all kinds of prayers and requests. With this in mind, be alert and always keep on praying for all the Lord's people. (Ephesians 6:10-18)

Although I would encourage you to pray however you feel led by the Spirit, here is an example of a daily prayer you can say in regards to praying for those who may come across your path today that may be a part of your Soul Goal:

God use me today to do your will for my life, that your will would be done on earth, as it is in heaven, through me. Whether it is through the work of my hands, words I speak, actions I take, or money I give, allow me to be highly effective in influencing people for your sake through the message of Jesus Christ. Open my eyes and ears to be sensitive to those around me that I may be able to discern those who are lost and need to know your message of salvation and grace. Bring people across my path today that I may be your witness to them. Give me courage that I may be a bold witness for you as you guide my steps. Allow me to speak in your power and strength and that the words I say may be effective in the mission you have called me too. I stand in the power of God, as a child of God, and come against any attack Satan tries to use to cause me to be unsuccessful in reaching others for the Kingdom of God. I declare that any attack from the enemy shall fail in the name of Jesus. Open the eyes, ears, minds, and hearts of those that you bring across my path today that they may be receptive to hearing your truth delivered to them through me. Thank you for the opportunity to serve you, Lord. And thank you for all those who will be saved by my actions as I seek to reach others for your glory. Amen.

Note: I also encourage you to pray for your fellow brothers and sisters in Christ. Pray that they would be highly effective in reaching the lost as well. Pray that they would be successful in reaching their Soul Goal and, if necessary, God would use you to help them reach it.

Determine to be a person anchored in prayer; pray for yourself and pray for others, pray when you rise and pray when you go to bed, pray in good times and pray in bad times, pray in successes and pray in failures, pray in peace and pray in struggles, pray in acceptance and pray in rejection... be a person of prayer.

Re-Evaluation and Reset

By now you should have a first year goal and a plan on how you are going to reach it. Remember, your Soul Goal is a life-long goal so once you finish your plan for the first year, you are going to want to create a plan for every year after that. With this in mind, I suggest doing a re-evaluation of your efforts and progress toward your Soul Goal periodically. In my opinion, you should at least do a re-evaluation once per year. A good time to do it is around Christmas or New Year's. However, you could even do a re-evaluation every six months or even quarterly (every 3 months). It really is up to you. The important thing is, doing re-evaluations of yourself will help you identify areas you are doing great in, as well as identify areas you may find yourself struggling. Furthermore, they are a great way to keep yourself as a Christian focused on the mission at hand in reaching others with the message of the Gospel.

What to re-evaluate:
Whether it was a 3, 6, or 12-month goal you had, look at your goal and evaluate whether or not you reached it. If yes, what were the objectives and actions you took that proved to be successful? If no, what were the objectives and actions you did, or did not take that hindered your success? Everyone is different and what works well for some may not work well for others. Identifying the areas in which you excel in your soul reaching or winning efforts is going to be a key to your success moving forward.

Repeat...

Once you reach the end of a period of time for which you have set a short-term goal for (whether a 3, 6, or 12-month goal), and you have re-evaluated your efforts over that time, set another short-term goal for the upcoming months or year. Based on the information you have on how well or not you did with your past goal, set a new short-term goal moving forward.

Determine what worked well for you and plan on at least repeating those efforts. You could even try to increase your efforts towards things that proved to work really well. Also, moving forward decide whether you want to eliminate or work to improve the efforts of things that didn't work well for you. Sometimes it easier to just eliminate your efforts towards something that doesn't work well for you and focus your time, efforts, and resources in a different direction altogether. Whatever you decide, remember, your intention is to always evaluate your efforts and improve upon them over time so that eventually, you are honed-in on being massively effective and efficient in winning or reaching souls for the Kingdom of God.

Many Ways to Win Souls

Multitudes, multitudes in the valley of decision! For the day of the Lord is near in the valley of decision. (Joel 3:14)

The point is, no matter how you choose to do it, make sharing the Gospel with others a priority in your life. Just because you think you may not be good at one method of doing that, doesn't mean there aren't other creative ways you can use to share the Gospel with others. Creating a Soul Goal and identifying strategies that you would like to use to reach it, is a great way to making your participation in the Great Commission a priority in your life and actually following through with your commitment to win souls.

In summary, here is what you have just learned to do in this section of the book: determine your Starting Point, set short-term goals by the week, month, and year, determine objectives you are going to complete to reach your goals, how to remind yourself of your goals and objectives, how to anchor your goals and objectives in prayer, and how to re-evaluate and reset your short-term goals. I want to encourage you today, you can do it. You can become highly effective and efficient in the plan and purpose God has for your life. Whether you follow the steps I just gave you to do that or not, strive to be on purpose, with passion, to reach others with the love of God and the message of salvation every day of your life.

Re-Evaluation and Reset

What is your Soul Goal? _____
(life-long number of people you want to win or reach)

How many souls did you reach/win (circle one) last
week/month/quarter/12 months(circle one)? _____
Did you reach your goal? Y/N
Why or Why not?_____
What can you do better?_____

How many people did you invite to church last
week/month/quarter/12 months(circle one)? _____
Did you reach your goal? Y/N
Why or Why not?_____
What can you do better?_____

Money you gave to missions last
week/month/quarter/12 months(circle one)? _____
Did you reach your goal? Y/N
Why or Why not?_____
What can you do better?_____

Amount of time you volunteered or worked at your church or other
ministry last week/month/quarter/12 months(circle one)? _____
Did you reach your goal? Y/N
Why or Why not?_____
What can you do better?_____

Number of people you called last
week/month/quarter/12 months(circle one)? _____
Why or Why not?_____
What can you do better?_____

Number of people you invited to a meal last
week/month/quarter/12 months(circle one)? _____
Did you reach your goal? Y/N
Why or Why not?_____
What can you do better?_____

Re-Evaluation and Reset Continued...

Number of people you brought to Bible study last
week/month/quarter/12 months(circle one)? _____
Did you reach your goal? Y/N
Why or Why not?_____
What can you do better?_____

Did you go on a Mission Trip this year? Y/N

Number of people you brought to church special events last
week/month/quarter/12 months(circle one)? _____
Why or Why not?_____
What can you do better?_____

Other (any other special events, programs, or ministries you gave
money to, worked at, volunteered your time with, or invited others to
go to) last week/month/quarter/12 months(circle one)?

_____

_____

Did you reach your goal? Y/N
Why or Why not?_____
What can you do better?_____

* This worksheet is intended to help you identify specific actions you
took and whether or not you or your actions were successful. It is by
no means a list of all the actions you could have taken...just a few
ideas to help you evaluate your efforts and progress!

Additional resources & more specific suggestions can be found at
www.SoulGoalBook.com

CHAPTER NINE

Keeping Records

Have you ever heard the phrase, "numbers don't lie?" Although we often like to think of situations or results as being different, usually better, than what they really are, looking at the numbers gives us a clearer picture as to what is actually the truth.

This is important because as Christians we need to know if we are actually being effective with our efforts to reach others or not. We shouldn't just hope and/or guess that we are. Especially when, understanding as a Christian, reaching others is one of the main reasons why you are still here on earth and a mission that God has given each and every one of us to carry out.

Be honest with yourself. Specifically define how effective you are in reaching others by putting a specific number to your efforts. Knowing how honestly effective you are today, will enable you to measure the increase of your success tomorrow.

There are several different things you can try to put a specific number to when considering your Soul Goal. Since missions and evangelism is specifically connected to winning souls, maybe you want to start recording how much money you give to missions and evangelism every year. With the idea that God is going to bless and increase you for doing so, make it a goal to be able to reach and increase your offering goal every year. Another thing you can do is keep an actual record of your progress toward your Soul Goal. See the Soul Goal Tracking Sheet in this book. Whether you keep track of your missions offerings, Soul Goal progress, and/or something else you want to record in regards to winning souls, try to put a specific number to it. In doing so, I believe God will honor your due diligence with eternal rewards and you will be able to see the blessing of God upon your life and the fruit of your actual labor.

Keeping Track of Your Soul Goal Progress

It is important for you to keep track of your progress as you work towards reaching your objectives, short-term goals, and ultimately your Soul Goal. I recommend, to the best of your ability, keeping track of the progress you make. Understand that you will not always be able to identify every soul that you reach, however the ones that you can identify I recommend that you write them down somewhere. This could be recorded in your personal journal or on a simple form like the one in this book. Here are some, certainly not all, of the reasons why I recommend doing this;

- God blesses those who are faithful with what they have been given.
- You are able to look back and see the fruit of your labor.
- It will motivate you when you are falling behind, and excite you when you are doing really well.
- And hopefully one day you will have to increase your Soul Goal because you reached it already!

Keep track of your progress towards reaching your Soul Goal. There may be times when you give to a missionary or ministry and it's very difficult to know just how many souls could specifically be attached to the money you gave. Or, you volunteer your time towards ministry work and it is difficult to measure how many souls were reached by your efforts. In these cases, I encourage you to do some due diligence to try finding out, if possible, the amount of people that were impacted by your efforts. But there are many times where it is simply just not possible to specifically know.

Nevertheless, as much as possible, try to estimate a number and record it in reference to anything, and everything you do towards reaching others with the Gospel. For example, you can at least record the number of hours you volunteered or the amount of money you gave. Record these numbers in your personal journal, on a Soul Goal Tracking Sheet like the one in this book, or on something else you create to keep track of this information. Keeping track of this information over time will enable you to look back and see how God has used you to reach the lives of so many. In addition, it will help you to better understand how successful you are in working towards your Soul Goal. If you never keep track of anything, it will be very difficult to know exactly how well you are doing in pursuing your Soul Goal.

A personal example to illustrate this concept:

Every year my wife, daughter, and I participate in a program called Operation Christmas Child, which is one of the many great programs through the ministry of Samaritan's Purse. This program sends shoeboxes filled with gifts all around the world, every year, to give out to children and is specifically designed to open the doors to evangelism. In most places, along with the shoebox gifts being handed out, there is a Gospel presentation in addition to a discipleship program for those children who choose to go through it.

At the time of writing this book, there are two different options people have for sending a shoebox, or multiple shoeboxes, through this program. You can either pack a shoebox with items you purchased yourself and provide an additional $7 to handle the shipping fee, or you can build-a-shoebox online at the Samaritan's Purse website by selecting items they have available online for a cost of $25 per box. For more info go to www.samaritanspurse.org

Ever since our daughter, Faith, was born, we have made it a goal to make at least one shoebox per month in addition to collecting these shoebox gifts through friends and family every year around Thanksgiving. Because my wife and I have committed to a family Soul Goal to reach a certain number of souls throughout our lifetime, we keep track of the number of shoeboxes we give. Remember, every shoebox given is a Gospel opportunity for someone to hear the Gospel through our actions.

Now, although there is no exact way of knowing, if we wanted too, we could make a conservative estimate of the number of children who accepted salvation by receiving the shoebox and hearing the Gospel message that we provided. We could then apply that number toward our overall Soul Goal. However, at any rate, even though we may never know the exact number of children who received salvation through our participation in this program, we at least know a minimum number of Gospel opportunities we provided based off the number of shoeboxes we sent.

Year after year we purposefully participate in this program because we have a Soul Goal established that we are working towards reaching. We personally record the number of shoebox gifts per year we send out as one of the ways in which we are taking action to reach our Soul Goal.

Think about it, last year maybe you gave money to a guest speaker at church, volunteered your time towards something or witnessed to a number of people, but because you didn't write it down, you now have no clue of how God specifically used you to reach others. Listen, if you can keep track of your bank savings account, how much more important is it to keep track of your soul saving account?

Once you have a Soul Goal, an important key to remember is this: whether it is the number of people you personally witness to face-to-face, the amount of money you give to missions, or the number of Gospel opportunity shoeboxes you send, make sure you record the information in order that you may see your progress toward your Soul Goal. Simply put, try to put a number to anything and everything you do towards reaching your Soul Goal and make sure to record it weekly, monthly, yearly or however you choose. It is a beautiful thing to get down the road of life and be able to look back and see specifically just how faithful God was in what you put your hands to do in order that others would be saved. In addition, this record would be a wonderful thing to be able to pass down to your children and/or grandchildren. It just may encourage them to have a Soul Goal too!

Note: As previously stated in regards to having a Soul Goal, there is a distinction between *reach* and *win* so let me further explain. Some people reading this book may want to set a goal for the number of souls (people) they want to *reach* with the message of the Gospel of Jesus Christ. Others may want to go a little further and set a goal for the number of souls (people) they *win* to the Kingdom of God. The difference is that setting a number for the amount of people you want to reach does not necessarily specify how many people you are trying to understand accepted salvation through you reaching them. However, setting a Soul Goal for the number of people you want to win, means you are setting a number for the amount of people you want to see accept salvation through Jesus Christ by your efforts.

When keeping records of your Soul Goal and your progress towards reaching it, have a clear distinction between whether your goal is to reach or win. If you choose to set your Soul Goal based off the number of people you want to win, because it is a bit more difficult to actually know the exact number sometimes, I recommend to keep track of the number of people you have reached as well. In other words, work toward your Soul Goal number of people you want to win and record every person you know you did win, and at the same time try to keep track of the number of people you at least reached, in your efforts to win others.

Soul Goal Tracking Sheet

What is your Soul Goal? _____
(life-long number of people you want to win or reach)

How many souls did you reach/win (circle one) last 12 months? _____
How many souls did you reach/win (circle one) last month? _____
How many souls did you reach/win (circle one) last week? _____

How many people did you invite to church last 12 months? _____
How many people did you invite to church last month? _____
How many people did you invite to church last week? _____

Money you gave to missions last 12 months? _____
Money you gave to missions last month? _____
Money you gave to missions last week? _____

Names of people you witnessed to last month?

_____

Names of people you witnessed to last 12 months?

_____

_____

Amount of time you volunteered or worked at your church or other
ministry last week? _____
Amount of time you volunteered or worked at your church or other
ministry last month? _____
Amount of time you volunteered or worked at your church or other
ministry last 12 months? _____

Number of people you called last week? _____
Number of people you called last month? _____
Number of people you called last 12 months? _____

Number of people you invited to a meal last week? _____
Number of people you invited to a meal last month? _____
Number of people you invited to a meal last 12 months? _____

Number of people you brought to Bible study last week? _____
Number of people you brought to Bible study last month? _____
Number of people you brought to Bible study last 12 months? _____

Did you go on a Mission Trip this year? Y/N

Soul Goal Tracking Sheet Continued...

Number of people you brought to church special events last 12 months? _____

Other (any other special events, programs, or ministries you gave money to, worked at, volunteered your time with, or invited others to go to) last 12 months?

_____

_____

* This worksheet is intended to help you identify specific actions you took to help you reach your short-term goals and ultimately your Soul Goal. It is by no means a list of all the actions you could have taken…just a few ideas to help you track your efforts and progress!

Additional resources & more specific suggestions can be found at
www.SoulGoalBook.com

CHAPTER TEN

Soul Goal Strategies

As a Family – Husband and Wife

One of the first things I did when God first started dealing with me about having a Soul Goal was to tell my wife what was happening. I told her that I felt God wanted me to give him a specific number in regards to how many people I would be satisfied with winning to the Kingdom of God if I was given the opportunity at the end of my life to look back. Out of curiosity to see what would happen, I then told her this: "how about you pray about a number and I will pray about a number and when we are both confident we each have a number, we will reveal our individual numbers to each other and see if they are the same or different."

A couple of weeks went by as we both individually prayed and sought the Lord for direction. Until one day, we decided it was time to reveal to each other the number we each felt God had given to us. I still remember the day it happened as we were in my office in-between patient visits. One, two, three as we counted down and then exchanged numbers. As we both looked at each others number, in that very moment, a mighty rush of multiple emotions filled our hearts and minds as we physically and mentally came face-to-face with the startling realization and revelation that God was going to use us to impact a greater number of people than what either one of us could have ever imagined before. In case you are wondering... the numbers were exactly the same.

I remember thinking that "I am hooked. God's got me. No turning back now. To do so would be to turn my back on God himself. He has unwaveringly pursued me for an answer. I have answered and he has now confirmed it to me." Even though I had previously had a sense of commitment to the mission of reaching others with the Gospel, at that very moment I had the strongest sense of personal commitment and responsibility in my mission as a Christian than I ever did before. A great sense of personal responsibility that persists in my life to this very day.

I say all that to tell you this, if you are married I believe you can pursue a Soul Goal together. Do you have to have the same experience as my wife and I did with individually coming up with the same number? No. And furthermore, if you try what we did and you both come up with two different numbers, I don't believe you should put any thought to who is right or who is wrong, or whether or not you should even pursue a Soul Goal together as a family. If you and your spouse desire to pursue a Soul Goal together or as a family, simply come up with a number that you mutually agree upon and start working towards it. Let me be very clear - do not ever allow the pursuit of a Soul Goal to drive a wedge in your family.

So, if implementing a Soul Goal is something you and your spouse mutually agree upon, the pursuit of working towards it can actually be a great way to keep your family centered around a common eternal goal. Furthermore, you can use your family Soul Goal as a way to individually build each other up in the Lord, encouraging and motivating each other to reach their God-given full potential in life.

Have fun with it! For example, I occasionally pick my wife's car up from her work during the middle of the day while she is working. I take it to get the oil changed, a car wash, or cleaned out. When I return the car to her work parking lot, I often leave a small note inside with a simple message to encourage her, build her up, make her smile, or just show my appreciation for her. In the case of our Soul Goal, I may right write a message that says something like this, "You are awesome. You just won many souls for the Kingdom of God today!" In this example, I am writing honestly and sincerely, as she works for a large international ministry. Whether her day has been stressful or not, when she sees that message it builds her up and lets her know I am right there with her on the same page of reaching our Soul Goal together.

Having a mutual Soul Goal as a part of your marriage can also help keep you from being distracted by other goals and things that could actually weaken, or even destroy your marriage. We have found intentionally making it a point to work together as husband and wife towards a common eternal goal in winning souls has enriched our lives and brought us even closer together as we pursue God's best for our lives and family.

My wife and I often make family decisions based on the Soul Goal we are pursuing together. Many times, when we consider whether or not the result of a certain decision is going to better enable us to reach our Soul Goal, or take us further away from it, it makes deciding what to do so much clearer. Just like you and your spouse may have mutual goals you are both working towards together for things like your house, retirement, savings, etc., creating a Soul Goal and mutually working towards it can be a highly effective way to help keeping priorities in line and your family centered around God and a common Christian mission and purpose in life.

As a Family – Teaching Your Children

Train up a child in the way he should go: and when he is old, he will not depart from it. (Proverbs 22:6 KJV)

Whether you have one child or multiple children, if you are a Christian, you can teach them about having a Soul Goal, too! In fact, whether you are a single parent or married and have a mutual Soul Goal with your spouse, consider at some point teaching your children about it and possibly including them in some way. I don't think it is appropriate to tell you what age you should consider doing this, as that decision should be made by you. However, if you have at least decided to set a Soul Goal for yourself, at some point you should consider explaining that to your children and answer any questions they may have in regards to it.

Teaching your children about your Soul Goal, especially in relationship to how and why you do things a certain way or make decisions the way you do, can be very effective in helping them to understand the core values, principles and mission you have as a Christian family. Furthermore, as you teach your children the value of setting goals towards other things in life such as reading the Bible, school, sports, church, career, etc; teaching them about a Soul Goal could help reinforce the importance of aligning their goals in life ultimately with God's plan and purpose for their life.

As a Church Family Together

Just as a body, though one, has many parts, but all its many parts form one body, so it is with Christ. (1 Corinthians 12:12)

An idea for the Local Church Body:

Much of this book is directed to the individual Christian simply because the mandate of the Great Commission is an individual responsibility for every follower of Christ. It is a humbling and awesome responsibility that we should all take extremely seriously: that God would choose you and I to reach his creation with his message of saving grace. However, we recognize that together we are the body of Christ. And even though we each have an individual responsibility to this mission, we should all collectively work together and share in each other's successes.

Two are better than one, because they have a good return for their labor
(Ecclesiastes 4:9)

Whatever happens, conduct yourselves in a manner worthy of the gospel of Christ. Then, whether I come and see you or only hear about you in my absence, I will know that you stand firm in the one Spirit, striving together as one for the faith of the gospel (Philippians 1:27)

With that said, the following is a simple idea that local churches may want to adopt in fostering the idea of working together as a church, yet keeping and promoting the idea of individual responsibility, to reaching others with the Gospel.

Step 1. During a particular church service chosen by the church leadership, members of the church are encouraged to fill out a simple individual Soul Goal form handed out to the congregation.

Step 2. Each member or congregation participant prays about and fills out their individual Soul Goal commitment for 1 year. This is the individual Soul Goal of that person. In other words, the number of people they are going to try to win or reach with the message of salvation in 1 years time. This is an individual commitment made by each individual who decides to participate. Every person may have a uniquely different goal number based on what they feel God is leading them to commit to.

Step 3. After everyone has filled out their individual Soul Goal form, the forms are collected and the church staff adds up the total number of individual Soul Goals to come up with a total Soul Goal commitment for the entire church body for 1 year.

Step 4. Once the Soul Goal number for the entire church body is added up, the church staff announces the total number to the congregation.

Step 5. (Optional) The church may then want to have certain church activities, such as Sunday school classes, outings, outreaches, or training designed to help and or encourage individuals to reach their Soul Goal.

Step 6. Re-evaluation. Periodically throughout the year, a re-evaluation of how everyone is doing in reaching their individual Soul Goal is taken. This could be a simple form that is handed out asking people how they are doing in reaching their goal. This could also be done online by the church sending out an email and having people take an online survey. The re-evaluation form could also include an area where they indicate what has worked really well for them, or what they may be struggling with that is preventing them from reaching their goal. Doing this may help the church identify areas they need to work on to improve, or areas that they are being really successful in as a church.

Step 7. Report. Once the re-evaluation is complete, the church may want to report how everyone is doing as a whole. This may further excite the people who are really doing a great job toward reaching their Soul Goal and also reignite a flame of excitement in those who may be falling behind.

And let us consider how we may spur one another on toward love and good deeds, not giving up meeting together, as some are in the habit of doing, but encouraging one another—and all the more as you see the Day approaching.
(Hebrews 10:24-25)

Note: I recommend the re-evaluation and report to be done quarterly. However, you may choose to do it semi-annually or other.

Additional resources including forms and more specific suggestions can be found at www.SoulGoalBook.com

Life Groups

As iron sharpens iron, so one person sharpens another. (Proverbs 27:17)

Studying the Word and sharing your Christian life with other fellow believers is a very effective way to grow together in the things of Christ. You may even do this now by being part of a home Bible study group, cell group, or Sunday school class. One great benefit of being involved in a group like this is having others to be accountable too.

Many people need accountability, especially when it comes to accomplishing their goals in life. I realize, some of you may want to keep your Soul Goal between you and God, which is perfectly ok if you do. However, sharing your Soul Goal with the people you are surrounded by in your Christian life group could be a very effective way to help and encourage each other in working towards reaching each other's Soul Goal. If you do this, you may just find having accountability to other brothers and sisters in Christ helps you tremendously. Also, this gives you the added bonus of everyone being able to all share in the testimonies of each other as you reach and win more souls. Watch out... Your life group may start growing!

Connect Them to a Church

Therefore go and make disciples (Matthew 28:19)

One thing you must keep in mind as you are pursuing your Soul Goal to reach and win others to Christ, is that the Bible says we are to make disciples and teach them about God. With this in mind, if you have the ability to invite the person you are reaching or winning to your church or connect them with a church in their area, try your best to do that. Remember, their new life in Christ has a really big family and whether they can come to your church or not, we should try to do our best to get them connected with a local church family and on their way to discipleship.

An Effective Way to Win

If you are going to reach your Soul Goal, it makes sense that you should know and utilize one of the most effective strategies to do that. I am talking about telling your personal testimony.

Telling your personal testimony to others is extremely powerful. It can be quite easy for someone to simply debate you about or refuse to believe the Bible, but when it comes to your personal testimony(ies) of what God has personally done in your life, that is much more difficult for someone to object to. For that reason, one of the most effective ways to witness to someone else about Jesus is by sharing with them some of the personal things you have gone through in life, and how Jesus has brought you through them.

You don't have to view witnessing to someone as proving to someone that their beliefs are wrong and you are right and once they understand that, you have "won" them. It's not a fight. It's not a debate. It is simply sharing with them how you and your life used to be without following Jesus, and how you and your life are now that you are following Jesus. Be real with them and share with them how your life has been transformed by the power of the Gospel. Talk to them about your personal relationship with God and how they can have one too.

Let the redeemed of the Lord tell their story (Psalm 107:2)

the Father of compassion and the God of all comfort, who comforts us in all our troubles, so that we can comfort those in any trouble with the comfort we ourselves receive from God. (2 Corinthians 1:3-4 emphasis added)

Think about it…spend time thinking about what God has done in your life. Think about how you may share some of those things God has done in your life with others. Knowing that your personal testimony(ies) is/are one of the most effective tools you can use to witness to someone, think about and prepare yourself to tell your testimony(ies). Simply put, use a personal testimony to be one of your main strategies to reach your Soul Goal.

Elevator Speech

But in your hearts revere Christ as Lord. Always be prepared to give an answer to everyone who asks you to give the reason for the hope that you have. But do this with gentleness and respect (1 Peter 3:15)

Many business owners, entrepreneurs, and sales people are familiar with the idea of developing and having a well thought-out Elevator Speech ready to go. I believe every single Christian should strategically develop their own individual "Elevator Speech" that they could give at a moment's notice, that is designed to have maximum witnessing potential packed into a short amount of time. Remember, once you have a Soul Goal, you want to take advantage of every opportunity that presents itself to get one more person closer to reaching your goal. Sometimes these opportunities present as just a quick moment in time to speak to someone and if you are not prepared ahead of time, you will 'flop' in the heat of the moment.

For those of you who are not familiar with what an Elevator Speech is, let me explain the basic concept. An elevator speech is basically a pre-thought-out response, communication, or interaction that you create and memorize in preparation for you speaking to someone in a moment's notice with only a limited time to tell them something.

In the business world, the concept is based off the idea of having a pre-thought-out response to someone you have just met when you step into an elevator, hence the name elevator speech. When the person asks, "so, what do you do?" - having an elevator speech prepared in advance will enable you to immediately start speaking to them in a way that is going to be most impactful, rather than you just stumbling around for words. Remember, on an elevator ride you only have a limited time to make an impact before the ride is over and the person is gone forever. Every word you say, and every second you take saying it, matters.

As Christians, I believe we should prepare ourselves in advance for moments like these as well. We have a far greater purpose in reaching people with the message of the Gospel, than any business owner or sales rep in the world has in trying to promote themselves, their business, or product. As you begin to set your mind and actions toward reaching your Soul Goal, I believe you will find taking the time to develop a good elevator speech will prove extremely valuable to you the next time you find yourself in a situation where you have a limited amount of time to share the Gospel with someone.

It is important to note that even though it is called an elevator speech, it is not intended to only to be used when riding in an elevator. The name just gives you the basic idea of the limited amount of time you have to interact with someone. You may find yourself in different situations all the time where you have a limited amount of time to have a conversation with someone. If you have your elevator speech prepared ahead of time, you can seize the moment with confidence, knowing that you already have prepared exactly what to say and how to say it. Being prepared builds your confidence, and having an elevator speech prepared and ready to go, just may be the difference between you speaking up or "clamming up" the next time you find yourself in one of these opportune situations.

In addition, remember, you can actually be the initiator of these conversations as well. You don't always have to think of an elevator speech as a response to someone starting a conversation with you. You can be the conversation starter. See examples below.

The best elevator speeches are ones that are developed by including facts, stories, or experiences that are unique to you. In other words, personalize your elevator speech to fit you. I have included some samples below to give you some ideas of what I am talking about, but I highly encourage you to put some thought into developing your own and personalizing it, or them, if you choose to create more than one.

You can develop several different elevator speeches in preparation for different situations. Here are some examples;

Ideas for types of Christian elevator speeches:
Do you believe in God?   You give a 30 - 60 second response based off your personal testimony
Are you a Christian?   You give a 30 – 60 second response based off your personal testimony
Do you go to church? You give a 30 – 60 second response on what church you go to and why you go there. Include an invitation to them.

Example Conversation initiated by you:

You: How are you today?

Them: Oh, I'm fine. or I'm doing great! or Today has been rough. or I wish today was over.

(no matter what their response is, you are going to follow with your pre-designed elevator speech)

You: Yeah, you know what? I just went to church yesterday (or whenever you last went) and the message was great. I left there so ready to take on this week and I can't wait to go back this Sunday.

Them: They may say many different responses here. It doesn't really matter what they say, just give them a few moments to respond.

You: Do you go to church anywhere? If not, tell them they should check out your church. Maybe ask them if they are a Christian. or If they believe in God?

Notice: The conversation that initially was just going to be a few seconds has now turned into a substantive conversation where you have given them solid information, and additionally opened the door for them to ask you for more information. Maybe they tell you they have been thinking about going back to church. Or they tell you they have been looking for a good church. Or they tell you that they are not a Christian and it opens the door for you to tell your personal testimony of how you received salvation. No matter which direction the conversation goes, having the elevator speech prepared ahead of time and you using it at the beginning of the conversation just turned what would have been a quick "how you doing? Fine. How you doing? Fine." conversation, into a conversation that could lead to this person coming to your church or even better, receiving salvation.

Conversation initiated by them:

Them: How are you today?

You: Yeah, you know what? I just went to church yesterday (or whenever you last went) and the message was great. I left there so ready to take on this week and I can't wait to go back this Sunday. How are you?

Them: They may say many different responses here. It doesn't really matter what they say, just give them a few moments to respond

You: Do you go to church anywhere? If not, tell them they should check out your church.

Notice: In both previous examples, whether you are the one who initiates the conversation or they are, you can use the same elevator speech to open the doors wider to communicating with them in an impactful way as a Christian.

There are many different types of elevator speeches and ways you can use them that I am not going to cover in this book. However, I highly encourage you to do your own research online on how to create an elevator speech and then begin to create one for yourself as a Christian on a mission to reach a certain number of souls in your lifetime. Just remember, when you start working on your own elevator speech as a Christian, try to develop them around the idea that you are using it to open the doors to witness, or share the message of Jesus with them in some way. Developing them around your personal testimony, favorite devotional, recent prayer time, and/or recent church experience is a great way to personalize them and give them a uniqueness that makes them authentically powerful. Remember, this is just one more powerful tool you can use to work towards reaching your Soul Goal.

A Practical Activity to Help You Speak to Others

Activity: if you have a hard time speaking to others about what God is doing in your life, practice speaking to them while you are alone in preparation for when you actually get in the real-life moment. Here is what to do… when you are alone in your house or car, just start having a conversation as if you were telling someone about what God is doing in your life. You could even visualize the person who is most on your heart. Or, you could just practice like it could be anyone. However, just think about things God has recently done in your life. Start sharing them out loud as if someone else was listening.

When you do this, you are causing your mind to be SET on the things of God. You will then find it much easier to speak to others because you will have some PRACTICE under your belt!

On a side note, doing this activity also helps you identify those things that God is doing in your life. When you start thinking about those things and speaking them out loud while you are alone, it will help to build your own confidence, faith, and gratefulness toward God. You will begin to see just how good God really is to you in perhaps an even greater light than you would if you never did this activity.

Call to Action (CTA)

The Call To Action (CTA). What is a call-to-action? A call-to-action is a specific directive prompting a specific response or action to be taken by whoever the call-to-action is given to. You have probably been exposed to many call-to-actions over your lifetime. Here are a few examples of what I am talking about:

Infomercial Call-To-Action: Most likely you have seen some product advertised on television with a quick 30 to 60 second commercial. In the commercial, they give you information about what the product is, what it does, what you will get, and most importantly how to get it. It is the "how to get it" that I want to focus on. Most of the time, near the end of one of these infomercials it will say something like this, "order yours right now by calling 1-800-xxx-xxxx." This is the specific Call-To-Action.

They have just given you a ton of information in a short period of time, but they strategically leave you with the lasting impression of giving you a directive of what they specifically want you to do, which in this case is to call the number and purchase the product.

Another example:

Online Call-To-Action: Many websites have specific call-to-actions as well. Most likely you have seen one as you have been browsing around on the internet. They are often near the "buy now" or "purchase now" buttons on a website. If a particular website has mastered the Call-to-Action technique, once the website has given you all the information they want you to know about a specific product, they tell you exactly what they want you to do, which many times is "buy now."

Now picture this, what if in either of the two previous examples they simply left out the call-to-action? Even though they gave you all this great information, they never told you exactly what action they wanted you to take in the end. Of course they wanted you to buy the product, but they never specifically stated to you what action to take to purchase the product. I think it is safe to say, leaving out the specific call-to-action would result in a drastic decrease in the success of selling their products. Not because the person didn't want to buy the product, but rather because they were never told what specific action to take to do so.

I think this is a valuable lesson we can learn as Christians trying to tell others about Jesus. Often times, you may find yourself giving someone lots of great information in hopes that they will be witnessed to and accept Jesus into their lives, however you never give them a specific call-to-action like inviting them to church, asking them if they want to pray with you, or even asking them if they want to accept Jesus into their life.

In every conversation you have with someone where the door has been opened to you to witness to them, always remember to try to include a very specific call-to-action identifying to the person an action that you would like them to take, or at least they should take, to implement the information that you have been talking about. When you do this, whether the person accepts your call-to-action now or later, they know exactly what they need to do.

God's Call-To-Action: Choose Life. As God's mouthpiece, you can give a call to action to others to choose life.

This day I call the heavens and the earth as witnesses against you that I have set before you life and death, blessings and curses. Now choose life, so that you and your children may live and that you may love the Lord your God, listen to his voice, and hold fast to him. For the Lord is your life

(Deuteronomy 30:19-20)

Soul Sensitivity - Urgency

In the examples I used in the Call-To-Action section of this book, I talked about the simple, yet strategic structure used in infomercials to deliver a specific Call To Action near the end of the infomercial. I explained how telling someone a clear and specific action to take is vital to the success of people actually taking an action.

Another important element usually found in an infomercial that adds to their success, is the element of urgency. If you have ever seen an infomercial before, you know exactly what I am talking about. Usually, in addition to a very clear call-to-action, they let you know there is a time-restraint to the offer. For example, you may not be able to get the deal unless you call within the next 10 minutes. Creating this sense of urgency to act now is a very successful strategy.

Did you know that there is an urgency to message of the Gospel as well?

He who testifies to these things says, "Yes, I am coming soon."
(Revelation 22:20)

Indeed, the "right time" is now. Today is the day of salvation.
(2 Corinthians 6:2)

I believe including a sense of urgency when we talk to someone about salvation is extremely important in determining how successful we are at it. Urgency as a Christian is important for a couple of different reasons. For one, the Bible seems to indicate do so. Secondly, you do not know how much time you have left in your life to tell others. And lastly, you do not know how much time the person you are witnessing too has left in their life to accept the message of salvation.

In summary, try to remember there is an urgency associated with others accepting the message of the Gospel. In addition, there is an urgency associated with your limited time to tell others, in an effort to reach your life-long Soul Goal during your time here on earth. Whether you pass away or Jesus returns before you do, know there is a time limitation to either of them and we must be urgent in reaching others with the message of the Gospel.

To the Business Man or Woman

Idea and challenge to any Christian business owner who reads this book:

At the beginning of each year, as you set the goals and projections for your business(es), include a Soul Goal for your business(es) as well. There are many creative ways you could do this. However, the important thing is, just try it out and see how God blesses you and your business when you do.

Here are a couple ideas...

- O Set a goal for an amount of money you would like to raise through special promotions that is going to be given specifically to ministry, missions, and/or evangelism.

- O Set a goal to donate a specific number of products and/or services to ministry, missions, and/or evangelism.

- O Determine a specific percentage, based off your sales or revenue goals, that is going to be given specifically to ministry, missions, and/or evangelism.

- O Any other creative idea you come up with...

Whatever Soul Goal you set for your business(es), just like with all your other business goals, periodically monitor your progress and take specific actions to keep you moving towards reaching the goal. Setting a Soul Goal for your business(es) is one way, in addition to your personal Soul Goal, to keep the other goals in your life prioritized correctly as well. Also, I find it an interesting concept to think that even our earthly businesses could build more than just earthly wealth, but heavenly wealth for us as well! The question is... how much is your business really worth?

Encouraging Others to Tell – The Compounding Effects of Multiplication

Notice the Great Commission is not called the Great Solo-Mission. It is called a Co-Mission for a reason. Why? Because we are on a mission together. Together as fellow believers and followers of Christ, and together with God himself. It is for that reason that I want to tell you to encourage other fellow believers to be the best they can be at reaching others with the Gospel as well. Encourage and build up one another in the mission of reaching others. Realize, you encouraging other believers to increase in their efforts to winning souls by setting a Soul Goal too, will have a huge compounding effect that will foster a great level of multiplication which perhaps you could not reach on your own. You activating or challenging other Christians to have a Soul Goal is extremely powerful, not to mention, another great way to work towards reaching your own Soul Goal.

One of the ways you can do that is by telling every fellow Christian you know to buy and read this book. Or better yet, you buy another copy of this book and give it to them as a gift that will have an eternal impact on them, you, and everyone that hears the Gospel because of them reading this book and setting a Soul Goal. I shamelessly make that suggestion because I fervently believe in the power of having a personal Soul Goal.

It is my honest belief that every Christian in the world should read this book at least once. With great humility, I hope for every Christian who reads it, this book is a great encouragement, help, and catalyst towards enabling them to reach their full God-given potential in winning souls for the Kingdom of God as they pursue their individual Soul Goal.

Make it a point to encourage other Christians to set and work towards a Soul Goal. An important key to reaching your Soul Goal is the principle of multiplication. Realize, when you encourage a fellow Christian to reach others...and they do it as a direct result of your prompting and encouragement, you have a part in every soul they reach! This is the power of multiplication!

In pursuit of reaching your own Soul Goal, make sure you encourage other Christians to start telling others as well. Often times, a friendly reminder or fresh testimony from a valued friend like yourself, is just the bit of encouragement a fellow Christian needs to rekindle their desire and actions to want to reach more people, too. Start asking other Christians you know, "what is your Soul Goal?" If they don't know what you are talking about, or have never set one before, explain what it is and encourage them to set one as soon as possible. Time and souls are of the essence.

Next-Level Soul Goal Thinking

Think about it: Jesus died on a cross and came back to life again over 2,000 years ago. From that point forward, even until today, people have been receiving forgiveness of their sins and eternal salvation through Jesus Christ. This truth is at the very core of the Christian faith. But how is it that people have heard this truth throughout the ages?

From the very moment of the birth of the Christian faith, people have been telling other people. It is as simple as that. Many people have died for simply sharing the message of the Gospel with others. Even in recent times we have seen our Christian brothers and sisters die because they were followers of Jesus Christ and refused to denounce Him. Nevertheless, it is brave and courageous Christians who take their responsibility to tell others about salvation through Jesus Christ seriously, who take up their cross, denying themselves and make it a point to reach others with this message throughout their lifetime on earth.

Some of these people have utilized their time on earth so well in this mission, that even long after their physical bodies have passed away, the work they did while they were here on earth continues winning souls with the Message of the Gospel. As a young kid, I was fortunate enough to have been raised in a ministry that was led by a man who did just that. The ministry of Dr. Lester Sumrall, LeSEA Ministries. My father worked for Dr. Sumrall for nearly 10 years and I attended his Christian Center School, along with many of his grandchildren from 1st through 8th grade. I have also at times worked for this great ministry. If you are not familiar with this ministry, it was and still is, a large international ministry based out of South Bend, Indiana which includes Christian television and radio stations, a humanitarian relief organization, and more. Dr. Lester Sumrall died in 1996 at the age of 83 years old. However, in addition to the many facets of his ministry already mentioned, throughout his lifetime he also wrote over 100 Christian books and teaching materials. Even though Dr. Sumrall passed away over 20 years ago, the fruit of his labor in writing books and building ministry outreaches continues to this day in reaching souls for the Kingdom of God.

I don't know about you, but that is the type of lasting work I want to be a part of. As you pursue your life-long Soul Goal, I want to challenge you to a next-level type of thinking. I want to challenge you to think about actions you can take and things you can do with your time now that will continue to keep reaching souls long after you are gone. In other words, try to find opportunities that you can invest your time and money into that will be a lasting work, producing a harvest of souls for the Kingdom for years and years to come, even after you have passed on from this life here on earth.

Additional resources & more specific suggestions can be found at
www.SoulGoalBook.com

CHAPTER ELEVEN

_____

What Holds Some People Back

My hope is that by now, you have decided that setting a Soul Goal is something you want to do. Maybe you have already set a Soul Goal and that's great if you have. Either way, in this next section I want to talk to you about some of the 'roadblocks' that hold people back from setting or working towards a Soul Goal. I also provide suggestions on how these 'roadblocks' may be overcome. Although there may be other viable solutions than the ones I provide, identifying and taking actions to overcoming 'roadblocks' is a powerful strategy towards accomplishing your God-given full potential in life. If any of the following 'roadblocks' are holding you back, whether you follow the suggestions I provide or not, as a Christian try to do your best to overcome them.

ROADBLOCK - Worldly Living

A Christian who continues to live no differently than they did before they were a Christian may have a difficult time seeing the value in setting a Soul Goal, and/or may have a difficult time accomplishing one they have set. Before you were a Christian, you used to follow the ways of the world. This type of living is most often self-serving and in opposition to that of a follower of Christ.

As a Christian, your lifestyle should be markedly different than those who are still following the ways of the world because you should no longer be following the ways of the world, but rather the ways of Christ. Living like the world encourages you to revolve your life around yourself. Living your life for Christ encourages you to place God first in your life and serve Him by working to reach others.

As for you, you were dead in your transgressions and sins, in which you used to live when you followed the ways of this world and of the ruler of the kingdom of the air, the spirit who is now at work in those who are disobedient. All of us also lived among them at one time, gratifying the cravings of our flesh and following its desires and thoughts. Like the rest, we were by nature deserving of wrath. But because of his great love for us, God, who is rich in mercy, made us alive with Christ even when we were dead in transgressions—it is by grace you have been saved. And God raised us up with Christ and seated us with him in the heavenly realms in Christ Jesus, in order that in the coming ages he might show the incomparable riches of his grace, expressed in his kindness to us in Christ Jesus. For it is by grace you have been saved, through faith—and this is not from yourselves, it is the gift of God— not by works, so that no one can boast. For we are God's handiwork, created in Christ Jesus to do good works, which God prepared in advance for us to do. (Ephesians 2:1-10)

If the way you live is a 'roadblock' for you…

Solution: Identify those areas in your life that do not line up with Biblically-taught Christian principles and uproot them out of your life. In all things, put God first in your life, instead of yourself. Begin to see the value in people and remember that we are all God's creations. He has entrusted you with the message of salvation to help you to reach those that are not saved. With this in mind, try implementing a Soul Goal to keep your mind focused on keeping God first in your life, rather than yourself.

ROADBLOCK - Doubting the Value of You

As a Christian, the value of your life on earth in your mission of sharing the Good News of God's grace to people throughout your lifetime is worth more than perhaps anything else you could value your life by. Simply put, the true value of your life on earth consists in the eternal impact you have in reaching others with the message of salvation through Jesus Christ. When you fail to recognize as a Christian that your life and what you do with it on earth really does have an eternal impact, you may have a difficult time understanding the importance of using your time to witness to others.

However, I consider my life worth nothing to me; my only aim is to finish the race and complete the task the Lord Jesus has given me—the task of testifying to the good news of God's grace. (Acts 20:24)

If you have a difficult time understanding why your life as a Christian really matters...

Solution: Recognize you have been given an awesome responsibility to tell others about Jesus. How well you do that has an eternal impact. No matter how effective you are in telling others about Jesus right now, work towards improving that over time. A Soul Goal is a great way to improve your effectiveness in this area of your life.

ROADBLOCK - Selfish vs. Surrendered Ambitions

As Christians we must recognize the difference between selfish versus surrendered ambitions. If you fail to ultimately surrender your personal ambitions to the purpose and will of God for your life, you will most likely struggle to understand how your mission as a Christian to reach others with the Gospel fits into your life. Consider this example:

John is a really good football player. In addition to his athletic talent, he has an ambition to one day become a professional football player because he wants everyone to know who he is and he wants to make a lot of money to buy whatever he wants. When he is in college, John becomes a Christian and life seems to be going quite well. One day, John eventually realizes his dreams and ambition and becomes a professional football player. Upon doing so, he does make a lot of money and becomes quite famous, just like he always dreamed of doing. However, when John became a Christian, he never surrendered his ambition to become a professional football player to the Lord. When he eventually became a professional football player, he used his success to glorify himself and never used the platform or money God had given him to share the Gospel with others. John made the critical mistake of holding on to his selfish ambition that he had before he was a Christian and never surrendering it to God to be used by him to win souls for the Kingdom.

As Christians, we must be intentional in trying to connect our own personal ambitions in life to God's plan, purpose and mission for us. Failure to do so will result in missed opportunities to reach people with the message of salvation.

If you have a difficult time surrendering or connecting your personal ambitions with God's plan and purpose for your life…

Solution: Identify the ambitions you have in life. Then ask yourself why you have each of those ambitions. Even if it is for personal reasons, try to find a way or understand how God could use you to reach others using the ambitions you have. In the example above, John could have still kept his ambition to become a professional football player. However, he could have surrendered his ambition to the Lord by purposing in his heart, mind, and actions to use his celebrity platform to talk about God and witness to others and/or use some of the money he made to give to missions, evangelism, or ministry work. This perhaps would have been easier for him to identify and prioritize doing if he had set a Soul Goal to reach others.

ROADBLOCK - Lack of Understanding

By God's grace and mighty power, I have been given the privilege of serving him by spreading this Good News. Though I am the least deserving of all God's people, he graciously gave me the privilege of telling the Gentiles about the endless treasures available to them in Christ. (Ephesians 3:7-8 NLT)

Yes, God has given you a personal responsibility to share the message of salvation and reconciliation unto God through Jesus Christ with others. However, you should consider it a great privilege that God would choose you to be the messenger of such a message as this. Failure to properly view serving the Lord in this way with your life as a great privilege, could lead to you having the wrong attitude toward reaching others with the message of the Gospel. As a result, you may be lacking in having a true desire to see others saved.

If you fail to see your obligation to the Great Commission as a privilege...

Solution: Remember that because someone else once took their obligation to reach others seriously, you heard the message of salvation. Think about how your life once was without Jesus and how grateful you now are that someone took the time to share salvation with you. Understand that you now have the great privilege to be able to do the same for someone else who is living a life apart from God and how you once were. It truly is a great privilege to be able to share a message with someone that can literally take them off the track to death and destruction and onto the path of eternal life with God. Understanding what a privilege this is will keep a passion burning inside of you to set a Soul Goal and take action towards reaching it.

ROADBLOCK - Fear of Failure

Fear, as it relates to the fear of failing when trying to tell others about Jesus, is not of the Lord. In fact, it is the devil who wants every single Christian to stay silent about salvation through Jesus Christ. Understand, as you commit to serving the Lord by telling others about Jesus, he will empower you with strength, wisdom, and courage. Many times, Christians become so intimidated and fearful of witnessing to others that they never experience God's mighty power, strength, wisdom, courage, and boldness that can come upon you as you begin to speak.

Solution: Like many fears and phobias, sometimes the best way to get over them is just by doing them. Step outside of your comfort zone and just do it. Try to find an activity or outing through your church where you are able to witness to others as a group going out into the community. Once you get more comfortable with this, you will find witnessing to others by yourself becomes much easier. Be determined to not let the enemy silence you with fear. Set a Soul Goal and be determined to reach it.

ROADBLOCK - Pursuit of Earthly Riches

Don't love money; be satisfied with what you have. For God has said, "I will never fail you. I will never abandon you." (Hebrews 13:5 NLT)

What good is it for someone to gain the whole world, and yet lose or forfeit their very self? (Luke 9:25)

The pursuit of earthly wealth is perhaps one of the biggest roadblocks that holds people back from engaging in the Great Commission. For many people, the pursuit of earthly wealth was their number one ambition in life before they were a Christian and unfortunately for some, once they get saved it continues to be what they spend a majority of their time thinking about and doing. They will do whatever they can to attain this illusion, which leaves very little time for them to think about and work towards reaching souls.

However, one simple thing you can do to help identify if you struggle in this area of your life is to think about how much time you spend thinking about money. If you spend more time thinking about money in regards to storing up earthly wealth, than you do about reaching souls for the Kingdom of God, you most likely place a higher value on accumulating earthly wealth for yourself than you do about reaching souls.

Don't get me wrong here. The accumulation of earthly wealth is not necessarily a bad thing, because simply put, it often takes a large amount of money to reach a large number of people with the Gospel. If your purpose in pursuing earthly wealth is rooted in your desire to reach your Soul Goal, being able to accumulate a lot of money may be a necessary thing for you to do.

However, if your purpose in pursuing earthly wealth has nothing to do with your Christian mission and obligation to win souls, your pursuit of earthly riches is most likely a roadblock in your life to reaching others with the message of the Gospel.

Solution: First, admit this is a problem for you. Set a Soul Goal, and start working toward daily, weekly, and monthly objectives toward reaching your Soul Goal. In doing this, over time you will naturally start causing your mind to think more about reaching others than you do thinking about accumulating earthly wealth for selfish reasons. In addition, any time you do find yourself thinking about building earthly wealth, it will more often be in regards to acquiring it for the purpose of reaching more souls and working toward reaching your Soul Goal.

ROADBLOCK - Failure to Accept Responsibility

Ask yourself from this very moment (looking towards the future): "Am I personally responsible for telling a certain number of people about the message of the Gospel throughout the rest of my life?" Are there a certain number of souls out there that God has given you the responsibility to reach?

Failing to accept responsibility as a Christian to reach others with the Gospel can be a major roadblock to fulfilling ones' God-given purpose in life. The act of setting and writing out a specific goal almost immediately brings a greater sense of responsibility to the individual who is doing it. Someone may be apprehensive to want to actually set a Soul Goal number and furthermore write it down because they simply do not want to accept their Christian responsibility to reaching others.

However, just because a Christian refuses to accept their responsibility to reach others with the Gospel, does not mean their responsibility to do so simply goes away or isn't there. In fact, one day everyone will give an account (2 Corinthians 5:10) to God for their actions on earth, including their individual responsibility to reach others with the Gospel. Realize, neglecting your responsibility in any area of your life usually eventually leads to a negative outcome. However, taking full responsibility to the mission given to you by God will eventually result in one day standing before God and hearing Him say, "well done thou good and faithful servant."

Solution: Use the principle of setting a goal and writing it out to fully embrace your Christian responsibility and commitment to the mission God has given you as a Christian to reach others with the message of the Gospel.

ROADBLOCK - Procrastination

From one man he made all the nations, that they should inhabit the whole earth; and he marked out their appointed times in history and the boundaries of their lands. (Acts 17:26)

"As long as it is day, we must do the works of him who sent me. Night is coming, when no one can work. While I am in the world, I am the light of the world." (John 9:4)

Whatever your hand finds to do, do it with all your might, for in the realm of the dead, where you are going, there is neither working nor planning nor knowledge nor wisdom. (Ecclesiastes 9:10)

You certainly did not determine when or where you were born, God did. He has a specific reason for you living right now in the exact time you are living. He has a plan and purpose for your life. As a Christian, that plan includes you participating in the work of the Great Commission to reach others with the message of the Gospel. Do not procrastinate about taking actions in life to do the work and the will of God for your life. You are a light in this world right now; however, know there is a time limit that you do have.

Solution: If you are a person that tends to put things off, do not allow yourself to do that when it comes to serving the Lord. Make serving Him the center of your life and the actions you take the reflections of your service, love and commitment to Him.

ROADBLOCK - Lack of Vision

Where there is no vision, the people perish (Proverbs 29:18 KJV)

Vision describes what you would like to become. How you see yourself in the future. Where are you headed? What will success look like for you as a Christian? You must have a clear vision as a Christian of how you see yourself in the future. Do you see yourself being a person who is a great soul winner?

Since we have been given the great privilege and mission to reach others with the message of salvation, I believe as Christians we should at least have a vision of ourselves excelling in that mission. Excelling at the mission God has given us to do. And if you were to excel at it, what is the vision you would have of yourself in the future being a person who excels in the mission to reach others? Failure to have a vision of yourself in the future that lines up with God's plan and purpose for your life can cause you to waste time and opportunities that God brings across your path to accomplish what he has called you to do.

Solution: Think about the number of your Soul Goal. Envision yourself one day reaching that number. Align your vision for reaching people as a Christian, with God's vision for them... *who wants all people to be saved and to come to a knowledge of the truth* (1 Timothy 2:4).

ROADBLOCK - Fear of Persecution

In fact, everyone who wants to live a godly life in Christ Jesus will be persecuted, (2 Timothy 3:12)

Living an authentic Christian life is not always meant to be comfortable, especially when it comes to telling others about Jesus. If all you do as a Christian is to constantly avoid feeling uncomfortable, while doing everything in your ability to never leave your comfort zone, you most likely are going to fail in your mission to reach others with the Gospel. I know that sounds harsh, but honestly it is the truth. However, knowing ahead of time that the actions you often times must take to reach others with the Gospel may require you to step outside of our comfort zone, will help prepare you for the opportunity to do so when it presents itself in your life.

The world wants you to seek after the always elusive position of comfort in life. As a Christian you must realize that sacrificing your own personal comfort in exchange for reaching someone with the message of eternal salvation is by far, worth it. Remember, Jesus has told us that we would be persecuted on account of Him. And guess what, persecution is not necessarily comfortable. So, don't limit your ability to reach your Soul Goal because you refuse to step outside of your comfort zone once in a while to tell someone else about Jesus.

Solution: Realize that God sees any persecution you may go through on the account of telling others about him. Spend time in prayer asking God to give you the confidence to be a great witness for him. Understand that God calls you blessed when you are persecuted for his sake.

If you are insulted because of the name of Christ, you are blessed, for the Spirit of glory and of God rests on you. (1 Peter 4:14)

CHAPTER TWELVE

Something to Think About

How Many Would it Take to Reach the Whole World?

Think about this: what would it take for every single person on the face of the earth to hear the Good News of Jesus Christ, if every single Christian became involved in telling those who have never heard about Jesus before? In other words, how many people would each individual Christian currently living have to witness too in order that everyone on earth hears about Jesus at least 1 time? It is quite an interesting thought to think about and the answer just may surprise you!

Let's do the math. There are currently just under 7.5 billion people living on earth. Out of those people, nearly 2.2 billion people are estimated to be Christians. That's close to one-third of the earth's population! Now, I do recognize there could be much debate as to the accuracy of the number of Christians, however for the purpose of getting a rough estimate and a general idea of this concept, let's just do the math with these numbers.

So, if we subtract 2.2 billion Christians from the total population of 7.5 billion people, we are left with 5.3 billion non-Christians living in the earth today. If we averaged out the individual responsibility to every single Christian to reach a certain number of non-Christian people in order that all Christians collectively reached the entire 5.3 billion non-Christians on earth, what would be the individual responsibility of every single Christian living today be? The answer… every single one of the 2.2 billion Christians would only have to reach 2.4 people in order for the whole world to hear the Gospel! Since there is no such thing as .4 percent of a person, let's just round that number up to another whole person. In that case, if every single Christian living today told just 3 different people about Jesus, the whole entire non-Christian population on the earth would have heard the Good News of the Gospel at least 1 time. Wow, what a thought!

Keep in mind of course, this calculation is based on the idea that no two Christians tell the same two people about Jesus. However, in terms of thinking about your individual responsibility to reaching others with the Gospel, I find this an interesting concept to think about and perhaps for some people, if nothing else, an initial baseline that they may consider in setting an individual Soul Goal to reach a certain number of souls with the message of the Gospel. In other words, could you in your lifetime, personally find and tell just three people about Jesus who have never heard about him before?

How Will the Greatest Harvest Happen?

I tell you, open your eyes and look at the fields! They are ripe for harvest.
(John 4:35-36)

I believe the greatest number of souls will be won in a given period of time when each and every Christian takes their individual responsibility in the Great Commission to reach others with the Gospel seriously. The day when each and every individual Christian makes a serious commitment to setting a goal to win souls, and furthermore takes daily action in working to achieve that goal, is the day in which we will see the greatest harvest of souls the world has ever known in one lifetime. When the goal to win souls becomes more important than any other earthly goals you, as an individual Christian may have, you will experience a power of the Gospel like never before. You will see God working through you to touch the lives of others in a most miraculous way. I believe the greatest harvest of souls to the Kingdom of God will happen through individual Christians in everyday life being totally consumed in working towards reaching a Soul Goal. If you're a Christian, that includes you!

You, as an individual Christian, have a responsibility to reach others with the Gospel. Are you doing it? The individual Christian must no longer avoid and/or ignore their responsibility. We must no longer dismiss our individual responsibility into the hands of others, such as pastors, preachers, evangelists, teachers, and prophets. Certainly, they have a responsibility to share the Gospel with others as well, but they cannot and should not be considered a substitute for your individual responsibility to this mission. For it is in the action of every single individual Christian responding to this responsibility, given to each and every one of us by God, that we will see the greatest harvest of souls the world has ever seen. I believe setting a Soul Goal and working towards accomplishing it with God's help is a starting point that every individual Christian can make as they commit their lives to seriously taking up their responsibility in reaching others with the Gospel. If you are to get serious about your responsibility, if you are to get serious about reaching others, get serious about strategically making soul winning a priority in your life. Setting a Soul Goal is one way to achieve this.

Fisher of Men

"Come, follow me," Jesus said, "and I will send you out to fish for people."
(Matthew 4:19)

To be a follower of Christ is to be a fisher of men. I love fishing. Ever since I was a little boy when my father would take me fishing, I have loved fishing. As a teenager, my brother and I would ride our bikes a couple of miles to the damn where we would often catch river trout and watch the "old timers" catch huge carp with their special bait they had cooked up at home specifically designed to catch these huge river monsters that would sometimes take hours to reel in. As an adult, I have continued to enjoy fishing and throughout the years I have learned a thing or two about fishing that also holds true when thinking about being a fisher of men, in other words, setting out to "catch" people for the Kingdom of heaven with the message of the Gospel.

Here are a few of the lessons I have learned about fishing:

Sometimes they bite, sometimes they don't. Sometimes you catch them, other times you don't. Nevertheless, you must keep trying if you are going to catch anything. There are times I have been fishing for hours and caught absolutely nothing. There are other times I have been fishing for a short period of time and caught a large amount of fish. However, I have never sat at home not fishing and caught fish.

The point is this, in order to even have the possibility to catch fish, you must go fishing. I find it is the same with being a follower of Christ and being a fisher of men, engaged in the Great Commission to reach others with the message of the Gospel. You cannot expect to just do nothing and "catch" people. If I am going to go fishing I must purpose in my heart to do so and take actions to literally get myself out there with a fishing pole in hand, casting out into the water. When you think about yourself as a follower of Jesus Christ and therefore a "fisher of men," purpose in your heart to have a personal goal to reach souls and then take action steps towards reaching that Soul Goal. Get out there and start casting. It may not be today, it may not be tomorrow, but sooner or later, you are bound to catch something, as long as you never give up!

Another thought to consider in regards to fishing. In some of the places I have been fishing, like deep sea fishing off of the coast of Florida, there are certain rules regarding the number of fish you can catch for certain types of fish. On these particular trips, there has usually been quite a bit of time, effort, and money that has gone into making the trip happen. So the thought is this: you want to catch your maximum limit of fish. In my experience, no one I have ever been fishing with on these trips has the mindset that they could just care less about catching their limit. No, everyone wants to catch the maximum amount of fish they can in order to make the most of their time, effort, and money doing it.

As Christians, shouldn't we have the same mindset? I don't know about you, but I want God to use me in such a way that I reach my maximum limit. If I compare my life to "one big fishing trip," I don't want to get to the end of the trip, my life, catching less than the maximum number I could have. From today onward, I want to have the mindset that I am going to do everything in my power, and with God's help, to catch my "max limit." As a Christian, I hope you have the same mindset as well.

Personal Struggles in Life

We all have personal struggles. Whether you are a Christian or not, we all have things in our lives that we struggle with on perhaps, a daily basis. Although others may struggle with the same thing as you, your struggle is still your struggle. No one can fight your struggle for you. Sometimes we allow others to help us in our struggles and other times we choose to fight them on our own. I don't know what your personal struggles are. However, first and foremost I would encourage you to give your struggles to the Lord. *Cast your cares on the LORD and he will sustain you; he will never let the righteous be shaken.*

(Psalm 55:22)

Above anyone else, allow Him to help you in your fight. Furthermore, try to re-align the reason for why you want to overcome your personal struggles, with your purpose in life to reach your Soul Goal.

I press toward the mark for the prize of the high calling of God in Christ Jesus. (Philippians 3:14 KJV)

Often, our personal struggles get in the way of how God wants to use us to reach others. We try to overcome our struggles for our own reasons, never looking at the bigger picture of how those struggles directly affect our ability to reach others for the Kingdom of God. I believe the more you can think about overcoming your personal struggles in the light of the awesome mission God has given you to reach others with the message of the Gospel, the greater determination and drive you will have to overcome them. Living for your own purpose and goals is one thing. Living for God's purpose and goals for your life is another. And no matter what personal struggles you may be going through, you are not alone. God is with you, so keep your eyes on Jesus, your mind on heaven, and your actions toward reaching others in pursuit of your Soul Goal.

Connecting Your Dreams and Ambitions to Your Soul Goal

Make The Connection...

Most of us have dreams and ambitions in life. Many times these dreams and ambitions are something you have had for a very long time, even before you became a Christian. Dreams and ambitions are important as they give us something to look forward to, something to work towards. However, quite often, when someone transitions from non-believer to believer in Jesus Christ, they fail to connect their long-held dreams and ambitions to their new-found purpose and mission in life to reach others with the message of the Gospel. They go on in life viewing their dreams and ambitions as one thing, and their responsibility to tell others about Jesus something completely different.

Understand that when someone receives salvation they become a new creation (2 Corinthians 5:17), some of the old dreams and ambitions you may have had will simply just not be appealing or even relevant to your new life now. On the other hand, some of those dreams and ambitions will still be very much alive inside of you because they were originally placed there by God. In either case, you must measure the validity and worthiness of your personal dreams and ambitions with what is found in the Word of God, the Holy Bible. Anything that you were pursing in life before you became a Christian that is opposed to, or out of line with what the Bible teaches, should be discarded and not pursued by you anymore.

However, the dreams and ambitions that were placed inside of you, even before you became a Christian, that are in agreement and alignment with what the Bible teaches, should ultimately be connected to you serving the Lord with your life by pursuing your Christian mission in reaching others with the Gospel.

For example, maybe before you became a Christian you had the dream and ambition to one day become a doctor. For as long as you can remember, that is what you wanted to do in life. Since you were not a Christian yet, you never thought of being a doctor for really any other reasons other than you wanted to help a lot of people and perhaps make a good living financially. But then, you received Christ into your life. You became a new creation in Christ Jesus.

However, the dream and ambition to be a doctor is still there. In this example, it is important for this person to connect their new-found mission and responsibility in life to reach others with the Gospel, to their dreams and ambitions in being a doctor. They must make the connection that they are no longer just pursing being a doctor to help a lot of people and perhaps make a lot of money. But rather, they are now living with such a greater calling to use their dreams and ambitions to help a lot of people and perhaps make money, but first and foremost reach others with the Gospel.

The fact of the matter is this, both a Christian and non-Christian doctor can help a lot of people and perhaps even make a lot of money, but if neither one of them tells a single soul about Jesus, the eternal result will be the same. No souls saved.

In this example, there are many ways in which the doctor could connect their dreams and ambitions to a Soul Goal. For instance, they could purposely set aside some of the money they make to give to missions work. They could personally go on Mission Trips where they are able to use their talents and skills to work on and witness to people. They could speak to groups of people about what they have learned in regards to the science and function of the physical body that God created, which would be a unique witnessing strategy coming from a doctor.

The point is this: no matter whether you are a doctor like the example above, or you have totally different dreams and ambitions in life, once you become a Christian, make sure to connect those dreams and ambitions to your purpose and mission as a Christian in winning souls. Do not make the mistake of viewing them as two totally separate things. For your dreams and ambitions as a Christian should realign to actually become a means by which you are able to reach your Soul Goal.

True Value of Your Time

What is the true value of your time?

In the developed, modern-day world a monetary value has been placed upon peoples' time. In other words, if I wanted too, I could pay someone an hourly wage for their time. Typically, we would mutually agree on a price based off the work being done and perhaps the experience the person has doing it. In the United States, similar to many other countries, there is even a federally mandated minimum amount I must pay someone hourly if I was to hire them. The point is this: people exchange their time on earth, time in their life, for money. Therefore, we could say that a certain person's time is worth a certain amount of money.

It is wise to know how much your time is worth. In other words, how much is your time worth an hour. Or perhaps, better yet, how much will someone pay you for an hour of your time. Of course you could say to yourself, my time is worth $100/hour, but if no one is ever willing to pay you that for it, it's kind of pointless to you if you are trying to seriously exchange your time for money. In other words, you will go hungry.

There are many different factors that go into determining what the value of someone's time is, such as educational level, experience, profession, etc. However, I am not going to go into all of that now. Why? Because most of them all boil down to one thing, what can, or does, this person produce with their time?

This leads me to the point I want to make and the concept I want you to think about as a Christian. If your time on earth has a monetary value placed on it based off of what you produce with your time, what is the eternal value of your time on earth in terms of soul winning?

Did you know... you can be earthly wealthy, yet eternally bankrupt?

Let me explain. Whether you are a Christian or not, if you spend all of your time on earth doing nothing but exchanging your time to accumulate earthly wealth, and you never use your time or that wealth for the benefit of the Kingdom of God, like winning souls, there may be no rewards for you in heaven. Likewise, the same is true even if you were born into great earthly wealth and you never had to work a single day in your life to make a living and you never spent any of your time or your inherited money doing good works for the Kingdom of God, like doing the work of the Great Commission. That's why the Bible tells us to spend our time here on earth storing up treasures in heaven, eternal wealth.

"Do not store up for yourselves treasures on earth, where moths and vermin destroy, and where thieves break in and steal. But store up for yourselves treasures in heaven, where moths and vermin do not destroy, and where thieves do not break in and steal. For where your treasure is, there your heart will be also.

(Matthew 6:19-21)

As Christians, I think we should not allow ourselves to only look at the value of our time from an earthly perspective. More importantly, we should consider the value of our time based on what we produce for the eternal Kingdom of God, not just by what we produce for ourselves here on earth. Ask yourself, how effective am I with my time at reaching souls for the Kingdom of God?

After thinking about it, if you feel you are not as effective as you should be, or would like to be, remember, the more you work at something, the more skilled you become, the more experience you gain, and the more effective you can be. No matter where you are today, decide that you are going to start working towards being more effective in producing not just earthly wealth, but more importantly, eternal wealth as well. If you don't already have one, setting a Soul Goal and working towards reaching it is a great way to start taking steps in that direction today and for the rest of your life.

Valuing People

For God so loved the world that he gave his one and only Son (John 3:16)

Do you value people? I remember the first time I ever saw someone die. I was in a foreign country working for a Christian humanitarian relief organization at the time. One night I was sitting in a car parked alongside a road, waiting for my driver to return. As I was waiting, a man walking down the street passed the car I was sitting in and proceeded down the road in front of me. Suddenly a car went speeding by and struck the man from behind. The man never even saw the car coming. To my surprise, the car just kept going.

As the man lay motionless in the street, it was quite clear the impact from the car had killed him. I began to ask the people who had gathered around as to why the car didn't stop, and furthermore, why didn't anyone go after the car to try to stop them? They began to explain to me that, in this country, people get killed all the time just walking down the road and most of the time the driver never stops and no one ever goes after them.

It was in that moment I came face-to-face with a difference of value placed on a human life. As I talked more and more with the people about this particular accident, I began to realize that the value they placed on the life of a poor villager just didn't amount to much. Up until that point, maybe I was a bit naive, but I had never considered that a life could be valued so little by other people. I had always been told that God values all people the same regardless of race, religion, color, or gender. That God made people in his image and he loved and valued each and every single one of them.

Understand you are valuable to God. People are valuable to God. And we must do our best to value people in the same way God values people. In working towards reaching your Soul Goal, try to see people the way God sees them; as highly valuable and loved. Loved so much so, that he sent his one and only Son to die on a cross for their sins. When we see people with eternal value, we begin to place less value on the distractions of this world and more value upon what really matters to God, souls.

Soul Sensitivity

"The Spirit of the Lord is upon me, for he has anointed me to bring Good News to the poor. He has sent me to proclaim that captives will be released, that the blind will see, that the oppressed will be set free, and that the time of the Lord's favor has come." (Luke 4:18-19 NLT)

To be sensitive too, means to have a heightened sense of awareness to something. I believe as Christians we should have a heightened sense of awareness to the condition of people (souls) that we come in contact with. I believe we need to be soul sensitive.

Furthermore, we need to have a heightened sense of awareness of what we are doing individually in our daily lives to reach souls. We need to think of going about our daily lives like we have an internal antenna or radar designed specifically to identify open doors or opportunities to reach others with the Gospel. Train your mind to have a heightened sense of awareness of opportunities in your life to share the message of the Gospel with those who have not already received salvation. I encourage you to have a heightened sense of awareness for those you may come in contact with each and every day that are lost, lonely, hungry, fearful, depressed, anxious, hurting, and dying inside without having a personal relationship with the Lord. Be on the lookout. Keep your antenna up and your radar working. Take action when you identify an opportunity to help others. Staying focused on your Soul Goal is a great way to ensure you keep a heightened sense of awareness, a sensitivity to souls.

What Happens When You Win a Soul?

"In the same way, I tell you, there is rejoicing in the presence of the angels of God over one sinner who repents." (Luke 15:10)

What an awesome thought to think about… every soul you win towards reaching your Soul Goal causes rejoicing in the presence of the angels! As people living on earth, even as Christians, I don't think we ponder enough about how our actions directly affect what is happening in the eternal realm of heaven. We are often all too consumed with only thinking about how our actions affect our lives here on earth. As you begin to pursue your Soul Goal, know that your actions go far beyond earthly ramifications. I want to encourage you today to make sure to remember and to rejoice with the angels every time you are able to influence one more soul to be a follower of Jesus.

Partner With God

You are my friends if you do what I command. I no longer call you servants, because a servant does not know his master's business. Instead, I have called you friends, for everything that I learned from my Father I have made known to you. You did not choose me, but I chose you and appointed you so that you might go and bear fruit—fruit that will last—and so that whatever you ask in my name the Father will give you. (John 15:14-16)

Did you know God is for you? Just think about that for a while.

God, the Creator of the heavens and the earth is for you. Look into the sky. Look at the trees and the birds in the air. Just think... the Creator of all, made this for you. He even calls you his friend.

To this day, it still amazes me to think that I am a partner with God in speaking his message of reconciliation, which is pure love, to his creation. Just to think about it leaves me in awe and wonder that my best friend is God and he trusts me, he trusts you, with the awesome mission to bring the message of salvation to others. The message that, upon its' acceptance will change the course of a person's eternal existence forever! Just think about that... that God Almighty Himself avails himself to me, to you, as my friend, your friend. If God is for me, who can be against me? If God is for you, who can be against you? I encourage you to approach working towards your Soul Goal knowing that God is for you. Have faith knowing that he is for you and he is going to help you reach the goal you have set.

The Christian 'Why' Test

One day, a Christian friend of mine was telling me about the prospects of his new job. He was really excited about it and our conversation went something like this:

Me: Why are you excited about this job prospect?
Friend: Well, because if I do it for the next 5 years consistently, I will be able to retire at a young age.
Me: Why would you want to do that?
Friend: What do you mean, why would I want to do that?
Me: Yeah, why would you want to retire at a young age, then do what?
Friend: I could do whatever I want.
Me: What *do* you want to do?
Friend: I don't know, but doesn't not having to work sound great?
Me: What's the point?

You see, what I was hoping he would say as a Christian, is that if he was able to retire at a young age he would have more time to do things for the Kingdom of God, such as witnessing or volunteering at his church, or at least say that he would have more money to give to missions or ministry. Simply put, I was hoping that his excitement in being able to retire early was rooted in his unique purpose as a Christian living on a mission for God to reach others with the Gospel.

I think it's safe to say that most of us have thought this way a time or two in our lives, myself included. After all, it is how the world tells us to think. And even though we are Christians, we are not perfect. Nonetheless, when making big life decisions like this try, to identify your purpose as a Christian in the decision that you make. Ask yourself this one question, does it help me reach my Soul Goal?

When at a crossroad in life and trying to make a decision about which way to go, in addition to seeking God's direction and getting sound advice from trustworthy Christian people in your life (like your pastor), asking yourself how each decision will affect you in being able to reach your Soul Goal may help you identify which direction you should take and which direction you should not. Ask yourself, will it be easier or more difficult to reach my Soul Goal if I make this decision or go this direction? You shouldn't solely base your decision off of this answer, however it may help you identify which direction or decision is better. In any case, whatever direction or decision is made, try to understand how your Soul Goal fits into that decision. While Jesus was on earth, he constantly sought to do the will of his father. In everything you do, seek to do the will of your heavenly Father as well.

"By myself I can do nothing; I judge only as I hear, and my judgment is just, for I seek not to please myself but him who sent me." (John 5:30 ESV)

Your Earthly Job... Do You See Change Coming?

Maybe after considering your Soul Goal, you are beginning to realize that you need to find a new job or career in life. Do not mistake what I am saying here. I am not telling you to quit your job today, tomorrow, or anytime for that matter. I don't even know what you do.

What I am saying is that maybe you find yourself working in a job that would actually go against your life now focused on reaching your

Soul Goal. Or, maybe you realize if you kept working in this same career path or job, it would actually prevent you from ever reaching the Soul Goal you feel you should work towards. If this is you, just as important as praying and seeking the Lord about setting your Soul Goal is, pray and seek the Lord about the current career path you are on, or the job you are working in. If God wants you to change directions, he will open and/or close doors and make the new path clear to you. Ask Him to do so.

Your word is a lamp for my feet, a light on my path. (Psalm 119:105)

When God has directed a change of direction in my life associated with a job or career, at times, it has taken up to a year to actually make the transition gradually happen. The important thing to keep in mind is this: if God truly does want you to make a change in direction in this area of your life, have faith to take the necessary steps to move in that direction. And remember, don't try to do it without God, do it together with Him as he guides and directs your path.

Word to the wise: If you need help in deciding what you should do in this area or getting ideas of what steps you could take, seek the counsel of you local pastor. *Where no counsel is, the people fall: but in the multitude of counsellors there is safety.* (Proverbs 11:14 KJV)

A Business Model for Success

Have you ever thought about what makes a business successful? Of course there are many reasons for success in business. Understand, you could write volumes upon volumes of books about successful business strategies and the like. And many people have. However, for the purpose of this book, I want to make one significant point here. Successful businesses master the discipline of setting goals. For businesses, setting goals is vital to their success. In fact, I believe businesses that simply fail to set goals, fail in business or at least don't do as well as they could if they had clearly defined goals to work towards. It's that simple.

As Christians, I think we should take note of this important strategy and discipline. Maybe we should individually adapt goal setting as a strategy and discipline to tell others about Jesus. It makes me wonder, if the lack of specific goal-setting is crippling to a company trying to grow and be successful, is a lack of specific goal-setting crippling to us as Christians in our mission to reach others with the Good News of Jesus Christ?

Recognize, our mission and individual responsibility to tell others about Jesus is far more important than the mission of any secular company on earth. If that is true, why wouldn't we individually at least use a vital strategy, such as goal-setting, in our personal lives to accomplish our mission that is so much more important?

You may even currently work in a job where you know exactly what I am talking about. Your job is driven by goal-setting. Maybe your employer sets a goal for you. Maybe you are the business owner and you set goals for your company and employees. You then do whatever it takes to try and reach that goal. If that is you, let me ask you a question: As a Christian, does it bother you that you spend so much time working towards reaching a goal for your employer or company on earth, yet you don't even have a Soul Goal to reach souls for Jesus in heaven?

I believe as Christians we can learn from this simple strategy for success that is utilized by most successful businesses and apply it to our everyday lives. Instead of simply setting a goal to achieve earthly success, whether it's for us or our employer, we individually as Christians can set a Soul Goal to achieve a success that goes far beyond our earthly existence. Reaching people with the message of salvation, a success that lasts for all eternity.

A Successful Mindset

Let us not become weary in doing good, for at the proper time we will reap a harvest if we do not give up. (Galatians 6:9)

One of the characteristics of wildly successful entrepreneurs or business owners is their mindset. The way they think. An attribute associated with this kind of mindset that I believe is a vital reason for many of their successes is their mindset and will to never give up. They refuse to accept failure. They always believe there must be a way around, under, through, or over any obstacle that comes their way, and they are going to find it. I believe Christians should adopt this same mindset about winning souls. In fact, the Bible says quite a bit about what we, as Christians, should "set our minds" on... *setting your mind on things above, and not on earthly things below* (Colossians 3:2).

A Portugal Story

In 2016 my wife and I, along with our little baby girl, Faith, took a trip to Portugal. My wife's parents, although they have been living in the United States for most of their lives, were originally born in Portugal. I have traveled to many countries, but I had never been to Portugal before. On this trip, we met up with my in-laws so they could show me the villages they grew up in.

One particular day, as we were visiting my mother-in-law's village, they took us to her father's farm. Her father had passed away several years earlier; however, the farm was still there... well, at least the farm land was still there. On our way walking down the little gravel road, overgrown with weeds and barely wide enough to fit a small little vehicle, my mother-in-law talked about how her father spent years and years working this land literally every day of his life. The farm was his life and it was beautiful. She described the luscious grape vines that he had carefully cultivated to produce the best homemade wine, the fruit trees that produced the sweetest of fruit, and the olive trees from which he made his own olive oil. In a very real way, his farm was his life's work.

However, as we rounded the corner walking along the narrow gravel road, we got our first glimpse of what was now the farm. The farm she had been describing to me was no longer there. Sure, the land was there, but the farm was so overgrown with weeds, dying grapevines, and buildings falling apart, that it was difficult to imagine what she had just been describing to me actually existed there at one time. The hard work her father had put into that land was all but gone. Of course, there were great memories of what it once was, but when you stood and looked at the reality of what it had now become, it was sad.

In that moment it made me think, "is what I am doing in my life as a Christian going to eventually fade away with time and be overgrown with weeds to the point that there isn't much that remains?"

As Christians, God's word promises us that our work on earth winning souls is an eternal work that is not done in vain. *Therefore, my dear brothers and sisters, stand firm. Let nothing move you. Always give yourselves fully to the work of the Lord, because you know that your labor in the Lord is not in vain.* (1 Corinthians 15:58)

In other words, the fruit of your labor in telling others about salvation through Jesus Christ will reap not only an earthly reward, but an eternal reward as well. Unlike an earthly garden, cultivating the soil of the eternal garden of life will result in the fruit of your labor being an eternal reward that doesn't pass away or become overgrown with weeds. I hope you can see the eternal value in working towards reaching your Soul Goal. In addition, one day when you are no longer here, I hope people looking at, and thinking about your life's work, won't see a piece of land overgrown with weeds or an accumulation of material things that you couldn't take with you, but rather see a great multitude of people that you reached with the message of the Gospel, a great harvest of souls.

God's Guarantee

Have you ever heard this statement before: 100% money-back guarantee? It is often used in reference to selling a product or service. In using this statement, the seller wants you to have confidence that whatever is being sold is worth buying. They want you to feel reassured that they stand behind the value and quality of their product or service so much so, that if you purchase it and it does not meet the standards of what was advertised, or you feel "ripped off" you can easily return it. They are trying to break through any wall of skepticism you may have that would keep you from taking action.

However, just because a "guarantee" is offered, doesn't always mean the product is good. Marketers will often use this marketing strategy to increase the sales of a product or service knowing that, even if the product isn't great, many times usually only a small percentage of people will go through the hassle to actually return the product and ask for their money back.

Do you know what the greatest guarantees in life are that you can be absolutely sure of? The ones made by God. That's right; God has guarantees for you and I. And make no mistake, if God guarantees something, you can be absolutely sure what you receive will be well worth it.

What are some of God's guarantees? First and foremost, God guarantees the promise of eternal life to those who believe in their heart and confess with their mouth that Jesus Christ is Lord. (Romans 10:9) He also guarantees the forgiveness or our sins (1 John 1:9) by grace so that we may be reconciled unto Him. Furthermore, God guarantees us eternal rewards in heaven for doing the work of the Gospel while we are here on earth. Reaching others with the message of salvation and discipling them in the ways of the Lord, earns us something far greater than earthly wealth. It earns us eternal rewards in heaven. I encourage you to spend time working towards your Soul Goal. Make it a part of your everyday life. And you can be guaranteed that for every soul you win for the Kingdom of God on earth, you will receive an eternal reward in heaven. It is God's guarantee.

CHAPTER THIRTEEN

Closing

In closing, I just want to say that even though this book is directed towards those who already call themselves Christians and have accepted Jesus Christ's death and resurrection as payment for their sins therefore, receiving reconciliation unto God, and the promise of eternal salvation, I understand there are people who could read it who have not already done so. If that is you, I would like to invite you to take that step now. After all, this book is designed to encourage my fellow brothers and sisters in Christ to set a goal to reach people just like you!

Know today, right now, you can have the assurance of eternal salvation through Jesus Christ and the forgiveness of your sins. It is God's gift to you by grace, as a representation of his unfailing, unconditional love he has for you. It is the greatest gift you could ever receive and the greatest decision you could ever make.

Jesus said, *"I am the way and the truth and the life. No one comes to the Father except through me.* (John 14:6)

Salvation is found in no one else, for there is no other name under heaven given to mankind by which we must be saved." (Acts 4:12)

God made him who had no sin to be sin for us, so that in him we might become the righteousness of God. (2 Corinthians 5:21)

If you declare with your mouth, "Jesus is Lord," and believe in your heart that God raised him from the dead, you will be saved. For it is with your heart that you believe and are justified, and it is with your mouth that you profess your faith and are saved. (Romans 10:9-10)

For it is by grace you have been saved, through faith—and this is not from yourselves, it is the gift of God— not by works, so that no one can boast.
(Ephesians 2:8-9)

Here is what to do:

Admit you are a sinner and the only way for you to get forgiveness for your sins is through Jesus Christ's payment for your sins by dying on the cross.

Believe in your heart that God raised Jesus from the dead and confess with your mouth that Jesus Christ is Lord.

Next Steps…

○ Read the Bible regularly.

○ Find a local Christian church and attend regularly.

○ Tell others about Jesus!

Connect with us!
Additional resources can be found at
www.SoulGoalBook.com

My Prayer for You

Whether you have just received salvation through Jesus Christ, or you have been a Christian for a long time...

My prayer for you is that as you set a Soul Goal, you will be empowered by the Holy Spirit in his might, wisdom, strength, and boldness; giving you courage to go after achieving your full God-given potential in reaching others with the message of salvation and reconciliation unto God through Jesus Christ. That you would daily set your mind on heaven above and not the earth below, charging forward in every good work that you set your mind to do in Christ Jesus. And in doing so, on that day, when your earthly mission is complete you will be full of the goodness of God, his grace towards you and others, and a deep sense of knowing that you ran your course and finished well, a living sacrifice to God and a life well-lived for the Glory and Kingdom of The Almighty God. Let it be so.

Final Charge to Thee

It's up to you
And it's up to me
Together with God
That makes three

Choose to run the race
And win the fight
With God's power
And in His might

YOU must choose
To take a stand
With the Gospel of Truth
In your hand

The Mission was given
And entrusted to you
A victory promised
But you must pursue

Take action now
Go win a soul
For the Kingdom of God
And with your goal.

What's Your Soul Goal … silly?

Joshua Heines © 2017

ABOUT THE AUTHOR

Dr. Joshua Heines is a speaker, author and evangelist who spends much of his time encouraging others that reaching their God-given full potential is certainly possible. He has been the first to accomplish many achievements in his family's history including: running marathons, speaking on television and radio, getting a pilot's license, and earning a doctorate degree. Dr. Heines has been involved in many different aspects of ministry throughout his life involving worldwide evangelism and extensive international humanitarian relief efforts. Together, with his wife and daughter, he gave up his private practice to pursue reaching an even greater number of people with the Good News message of Jesus Christ. He and his family remain fully committed to their life-long Soul Goal.

Check out our additional resources at

www.SoulGoalBook.com

- Meet the Author
- Soul Goal Certificate
- Additional forms
- Videos
- Blog Posts
- Social
- More…

Orders By The Case Are Available And Highly Suggested For Your Church, Group or Friends and Family!

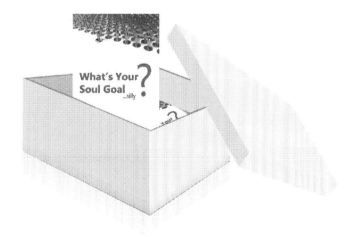

Made in the USA
Charleston, SC
24 February 2017